The Behind-the-Scenes Story of
WOODSTOCK

LOVE

Young Men With Unlimited Capital

With a New Introduction for the
20th-Anniversary Edition

el Rosenman, John Roberts and Robert Pilpel

YOUNG MEN WITH UNLIMITED CAPITAL

YOUNG MEN WITH UNLIMITED CAPITAL

Joel Rosenman
John Roberts
Robert Pilpel

A
BANTAM
TRADE
PAPERBACK

BANTAM BOOKS
NEW YORK · TORONTO · LONDON · SYDNEY · AUCKLAND

This edition contains the complete text of the original hardcover edition.
NOT ONE WORD HAS BEEN OMITTED.

YOUNG MEN WITH UNLIMITED CAPITAL
A Bantam Book / published by arrangement with the authors.

PRINTING HISTORY
Harcourt Brace Jovanovich edition published 1974
Bantam edition / August 1989

"Woodstock" is a registered trademark of Woodstock Ventures.

Library of Congress Cataloging-in-Publication Data

Rosenman, Joel.
  Young men with unlimited capital / Joel Rosenman, John Roberts, Robert Pilpel. — Bantam ed.
      p.   cm.
  Reprint. Originally published: New York : Harcourt Brace Jovanovich, 1974.
    ISBN 0-553-34729-2
    1. Woodstock Festival, Woodstock, N.Y., 1969.
  I. Roberts, John (John Peter)   II. Pilpel, Robert H.
  III. Title.
    [ML38.W66R67   1989]
  782.42166'079'74734—dc20

                                                                88-43337
                                                                    CIP
                                                                    MN

Published simultaneously in the United States and Canada

Bantam Books are published by Bantam Books, a division of Bantam Doubleday Dell Publishing Group, Inc. Its trademark, consisting of the words "Bantam Books" and the portrayal of a rooster, is Registered in U.S. Patent and Trademark Office and in other countries. Marca Registrada. Bantam Books, 666 Fifth Avenue, New York, New York 10103.

PRINTED IN THE UNITED STATES OF AMERICA

FG   0 9 8 7 6 5 4 3 2 1

HOW IT HAPPENED

For three years Bob Pilpel wrote Yale Law School chum Rosenman long letters asking, pleading, demanding that Rosenman put his Woodstock experiences down on paper. Pilpel offered to bring to the project his own budding talents as catalyst, co-author, and slave driver. When he sweetened the confection by providing an interested publisher, Rosenman and partner, Roberts, could no longer resist.

In addition to gathering a scattered wealth of source materials, authoring the third-person anecdotes, and editing, Pilpel somehow managed to keep Rosenman and Roberts at their typewriters. What follows is the result.

CONTENTS

Almost twenty years ago, on the weekend when the Wood-stock Generation got its name, we were sitting in a construction trailer at the Festival site, wondering how things could have gotten so far out of hand. A line of people stretched out the door and around the block, each standee waiting politely for his turn to scream complaints at us. As we write this introduction to the 1989 edition we are in the middle of planning a second entertainment event that, we expect, will give the original Woodstock a run for its money. After reading this book, with full knowledge that we intend to produce another Woodstock, you may conclude that our brains have been formed without the benefit of the basic food groups.

When this book was originally published, the memory of the roller coaster ride we took at Woodstock had softened. And to the rest of the world, Woodstock had come to stand for the sixties: a last gasp of romantic innocence. Indeed, in the mid-seventies, innocence was in short supply: corruption in high places, oil shocks, and a self-centered, often cynical, view of the universe had come together to define something called the Me Generation.

And by the mid-seventies rock festivals, in particular, had been tarnished by greedy, and sometimes unscrupulous, promoters, unruly crowds, and sky-high fees for performers. Rock and roll had become such a big business that there no longer seemed to be a place for a homemade festival like Woodstock.

So we moved ahead with our own lives and turned our attention to the ups and downs of more conservative business careers. Our families sprang up around us, seemingly overnight. We tucked Woodstock away in our scrapbooks and stayed out of the newspapers. We kept the trademarks warm and took care that no one came out with Woodstock brand edible lingerie.

Fast-forward to 1989. Many of the rock stars of twenty years ago are still the stars of today, and the fascination with the counterculture of the sixties seems to be more intense than ever. Anyone who keeps up with the news knows that Woodstock has become timeless. It has turned out to be more than just the good old days for those who were there and those who felt they were there.

Nowadays, trying to analyze Woodstock is like trying to figure out what has happened to civilization in the latter half of the twentieth century. Back in sixty-nine we sent out invitations to a rock and roll party in the clean country air. Thousands were invited—millions tried to attend. When we looked around us that weekend in White Lake, we were astonished to discover that we were a "generation"—bound together by more than just a love of music. We had come into the world with a self-centered mission: eat, sleep, have some fun, make a few bucks. Then at Woodstock we stumbled upon a powerful resource: community. These two elements, self and community, often clash as we go through life. When they do, the results read like a police blotter of the last twenty years: Watergate, insider trading, Iranscam, and the destruction-for-profit of the planet's ecosystem. But when these two elements harmonize, they yield miracles: team-work, heroism, diplomacy, and love.

Twenty years after the miracle of sixty-nine, the world still loves to party. We come to 1989 full of fun and a great willing-ness to kick off our shoes. We dance, we sing, we celebrate with our friends, and the world edges back from the abyss of nuclear war. We form a conga line, chant R&B, and soon a huge number of us want to draw the line against ecological suicide. We don't know how this happens. We know only that together in this music, we feel as if we are together on this planet—that our children and your children and their children are all *our* children.

There are hopeful signs. The rock and roll community is in the forefront of efforts to bring the world's resources to the battle for worldwide well-being. This awareness of our global community might be the greatest achievement of the Woodstock generation—perhaps it grew, in part, from what was sown in Max Yasgur's field that summer. So we are planning another party.

The ideas have been pouring in. We've been told to rent some barges, tie them together, and float a couple hundred thousand people and musicians around New York harbor. We've been advised to rent a meteor crater ("the best natural amphitheater in the world") in Arizona and fill it with a million people. And, of course, no need to bother with rain insurance for that site. We considered an abandoned naval airbase. There we found abundant space, but a military-industrial miasma floats like a sigh over the runways. Most proposers urge us just to rent a field somewhere—anywhere—and tack up a sign that says Woodstock: millions of feet will beat a path to our door, and millions of their dollars will flow into the Woodstock Festival Foundation. But something about that one doesn't satisfy us: the Foundation is a worthy cause, but the next Woodstock has to be more than only an echo of the past.

It's not easy to find just the right thing to do. But it can be fun. A few weeks ago we were visited by Jimmy Smith, an Australian aborigine on a diplomatic mission. He asked us if it was okay to lean his didgeridoo against our laser printer. A didgeridoo is a native Australian instrument that started life as the limb of a tree. A laser printer eats some forest products, but not didgeridoos. Jimmy Smith seemed quite at home in the office of J.R. Capital Corp. He favored us with a warm smile. He had been selected by his tribe to bring us an encouraging message: Civilization, as we know it, is on the brink of a revolutionary change. Woodstock was the signal of this change—the most important single event in the last two hundred years of the white man's history. The next Woodstock, stated Mr. Smith, will accelerate that change, and when the New Age has dawned, the world will be united in peace, prosperity, and love.

He closed his presentation by blowing his didgeridoo. It made a deep, important sound, the sound an ocean liner might make as it steamed into your living room. Finally, Mr. Smith offered to recruit a thousand didgeridoo players to perform at the next great Woodstock.

We're going to hold out for the right idea, no matter how long it takes. We hope Jimmy Smith is a part of that idea. It may not happen in 1989, but it will happen soon—every generation should have a Woodstock of its own.

We have some thoughts about this book itself. For example, upon rereading it, we're sure we could not have been as dumb as we appear. In any event, the book is forbidden in our own households until our children are safely launched on their own, more prudent careers in neurosurgery, haberdashery, or whatever.

For the two of us, haberdashery is probably no longer an option. But we are excited about the plans we have for the future. We remain best of friends and the best of sparring partners. That hasn't changed in twenty years. We find ourselves in agreement now that bringing Woodstock to a new generation is our main mission—which probably means that neither of our elevators is reaching the top floor these days.

There's a saying: Few partnerships can survive great success or great failure. Ours has survived Woodstock. You may draw your own conclusions about that and us when you finish the book. We hope you enjoy reading it as much as we enjoyed editing each other's best lines.

Joel Rosenman
John Roberts

February 15, 1989

Introduction

White Lake, New York
Sunday, August 17, 1969, 11:30 P.M.

The rain has stopped; one of those snide meteorological ironies, like the sky clearing just after your picnic's been ruined. Three miles away the biggest picnic of them all is still in progress, however, and the sounds of the celebrations drift down through the chill dampness into the quiet streets.

A green Porsche backs onto State Route 17B, faces east, and idles while the driver puts out one cigarette and lights another. His companion sits silent, his eyes empty of everything but fatigue.

Outside the town some of the weekend's debris becomes visible in the beam of the headlights. Parked—or abandoned—cars dot the roadside. Litter covers mud. Mud covers litter. Headed in the opposite direction, a wrecker roars by, a "modified" Cadillac hearse in tow. The passenger in the Porsche laughs grimly to himself: an omen.

Near Monticello a sullen bedraggled girl sits at the feet of a young man with a Jewish Afro and a beard who is soliciting a ride. As the Porsche approaches, the mouth beneath the hair is smiling and the message "We are all brothers" illuminates the eyes. But the car does not decelerate and the smile freezes. In the rearview mirror it has become a snarl framing an outstretched fist, middle finger up.

Three days of Peace and Music are ending.

It is nearly midnight as the Porsche turns onto the four-lane Route 17, a road called the New York Quickway; another nasty irony in light of the last seventy-two hours. The car picks up speed and the wind coming through the partially open windows rustles a copy of the Sunday *News* which is lying on the back seat. "HIPPIES MIRED IN SEA OF MUD" is the front-page banner.

"Jesus!" says the driver after a few miles.

"Did you ever dream you threw a party, and nobody came?"

For some time they reflect on this in silence.

"We must be at least half a million overdrawn," says the driver.

"The Bank is nine o'clock tomorrow?"

"Nine o'clock today," the passenger repeats numbly. "Time sure passes quickly on the Quickway."

They reach the New York Thruway and head south.

"Joel, do you remember, in March or whenever it was?"

"Remember what?" the passenger replies after some moments.

"You know: when you were so discouraged about everything."

"Oh, yeah, I was going to take a year off or something. Find myself."

"Right. You remember what you said? Famous last words: 'You're well on your way, Jock. You've got a good project. . . .' "

"And good partners. I remember saying good partners. 'You don't need me. You've got Michael and Artie.' Wow!"

"What was it Artie was screaming for today? Two cases of Coca-Cola for Blood Sweat and Tears. Immediately! By helicopter!"

"Damn the expense, man! The talent is thirsty."

"Damn the expense, man! It's not our money."

The laugh.

"And Michael: 'Hey, Joel, this is really a heavy trip, man! You gotta come up here and see this.' 'Sure Michael. Right away. On my lunch break.' Christ!"

The Porsche is crossing the Tappan Zee Bridge. Halfway across the span, at its highest point above the river, the sky to the south can be seen glowing dully. New York.

"Well, Jock," encourages the passenger, "it'll be something to tell our grandchildren about."

"Yeah. As we huddle together for warmth on the bread line."

"Bread line, hell. When they come to visit us in prison."

Conversation ceases.

Then, with a note of angry desperation. "Shit, Joel! What are we going to do?"

"I don't know, Jock. More important is what's the Bank going to do. What's Lefkowitz going to do? What's Warner Brothers going to do?"

"Warner Brothers! Jesus! I hope they had film in those cameras."

They fall silent again. The car moves quickly along the Major Deegan Expressway, then across the Triboro Bridge and down the FDR Drive. At 86th and Lexington the passenger leaps out to buy a *Times* at an all-night newsstand. He re-enters the car with the part open to the editorial page.

"Well?" asks the driver.

"It's headed 'NIGHTMARE IN THE CATSKILLS.' You need to hear more?"

"In the Catskills, my foot! They ought to join us at the Bank in seven hours, they want to talk about nightmares."

The passenger grimaces. "Well, the nightmare idea has one advantage. Sooner or later we've got to wake up."

"That's what worries me most," says the driver as he turns in to their apartment building's garage. "What if we wake up dead?"

John (Jock) Roberts on Himself

The difference between me and most other poor little rich kids is that I got my hands on my money at the relatively early age of twenty-one. Thus, graduation from the University of Pennsylvania in May of 1966 thrust me out into the world fully equipped to lead the life of an eighteenth-century country squire. I did have one or two minor problems, however, the first of which was a scarcity of job openings for millionaire history majors with B-minus averages. I mean, with several million dollars coming your way, would you want to start off in the mail room at the old man's firm? I dealt with that problem by joining the Reserves and enrolling in the Annenberg School of Communications in Philadelphia. The Reserves kept me from disgracing my class by being drafted and the communications curriculum kept me from making any rash commitments to a career.

But I come from a Jewish family, and, like Jewish families the world over, it takes the living and earning processes very seriously and has very definite standards of right and wrong. Futzing around in college clearly wasn't right, for example, and not having a plan for after graduation was definitely WRONG. Worse still, deep in my gut I agreed with these judgments, but what was the point of working hard to earn money when I already had more money than most people earn in a lifetime?

I couldn't take much solace in the example of my father. When he married my mother, he was taken into my grandfather's extensive pharmaceutical business and gradually worked his way up to the position of co-president with my uncles. Then, when my mother died, I became rich by force of her will while my father fell out with her brothers and found himself unemployed at the age of forty-eight. All he did then was spend fifteen grinding years building up a company of his own, and succeeding. In doing so, he proved something to himself about his ability and his integrity as a man, and I guess he stood in my mind as a combination reproach and example. For good or ill, I was stuck with the conviction that I couldn't spend my life lolling around in luxury and still retain any self-respect, and out of that conviction came my association with Joel, the business ventures we plunged into together, and Woodstock.

Joel (Joel) Rosenman on Himself

Most folks think that when you get out of college and graduate school and you move to the big city, things will take a turn for the sophisticated. I didn't. As far as I was concerned, I had been right in the thick of things all through my university career. I had done some nightclub singing—pretty heavy stuff. I had tried to haggle with some of the sharpest entertainment managers on the East Coast and in Las Vegas. I had dated some women fast enough to frighten me. I had even gotten drunk once.

I had known adversity, too. During my last year at Yale Law School, for example, a prominent Long Island orthodontist who also chanced to be my father determined that my bite was ready for alterations and proceeded to set up a machine-tool foundry in my mouth. With rubber bands for my tongue to play with, the tiny amount of concentration I had for my studies vanished completely. I accordingly was forced to regard my first attempt at the New York Bar exam as simply a warm-up, but, *mirabile dictu*, I passed . . . with flying braces. This astounding success left me with a blank for a future, *i.e.*, the legal profession and my uncle's prospering law firm beckoned.

I decided to take a week or two out at the ancestral halls in

Huntington before embarking upon my career. I was joyously received and treated for a period of time (three hours or so) with all the deference due a son who has left home as a high-school student with extensive experience in lawn-mowing and life-guarding and returned a full-fledged lawyer. During the first few minutes of the fourth hour, however, old habits began to prevail. I started to itch in places that hadn't irritated me for years. I took to spending afternoons on a sun chaise in the back yard. It was August and hot.

We had always lived in the same house; this had always been my back yard. At age five I had stumbled around out here, a frail asthmatic kid trying to keep up with a younger and effortlessly athletic brother. By age thirteen my inventory of afflictions disappeared, leaving me bookish and tubby. By age fifteen, just as scholastics and sarcasm seemed to be the only fields left for me, I molted, ending up in my present roughly humanoid condition. A facility with words that undoubtedly has already captured the reader's admiration led me to the English Literature Department at Princeton, which, of course, leads nowhere. And so I had gone on to law school, as a result of which I knew my rights.

If my folks had known that my meeting John Roberts would sound the knell for my career in the family firm, they probably would have slipped something into my Wheaties that August day when my brother, Douglas, brought him out to the house. I got safely through breakfast, however, introductions were made, and the three of us headed out for a bogeyful round of golf.

You can tell a lot about a man watching him duck-hook his tee shots, shank his fairway irons, and knock his putts off the green, and so I learned more than I needed to know about "Jocko" Roberts that afternoon. When we discovered that, in addition to complementary neuroses, we also shared an intention to get apartments in the city, the conclusion seemed preordained. Within six months I had quit the family firm, Jock had quit graduate school, and we were, speaking very loosely, well on our way.

Lang and Kornfeld: First Encounter

Apartment 32-C, 185 East 85th Street, Manhattan
Thursday, February 6, 1969, 3:00 P.M.

Mike Lang and Artie Kornfeld have an interesting idea they'd like to discuss. That is what Artie's lawyer, Miles Lourie, has told Joel and John.

"Now listen," Miles had said to them over the phone, "don't be put off by these guys' appearance. They may look a little unusual, but they're not dummies."

Kornfeld, they were told, was head of Contemporary Product at Capitol Records and the erstwhile producer of the Cowsills. Lang had had a hand in the organization of the Miami Pops Festival and managed a group called Diesel.

"Just hear them out," Miles had said as the conversation was ending. "Just listen to what they have in mind. It won't cost you anything."

Mike and Artie enter the apartment. Introductions are made.

Joel and John exchange a quick glance. Their visitors, particularly Lang, do indeed look "a little unusual" to them. Kornfeld has longish brown hair and is wearing an embroidered leather vest over a T shirt. Fair enough. Lang, however, cannot be placed on the spectrum. An enormous halo of dark curls frames a face that is, by turns, evil, wanton, fey, impish, and innocent. Beneath this disturbingly protean countenance: a frayed work shirt, an Indian leather belt, faded Levi's, cracked and filthy cowboy boots.

There isn't time to register astonishment. On introducing himself and Lang, Kornfeld grasps first John's, then Joel's, hand in both of his and smiles a smile of fraternal commiseration, as though he and they share some painful secret or are about to embark on a dangerous mission behind enemy lines. Lang is cheerfully acquiescent, all-accepting, attuned to unknowable vibrations. Without quite knowing how it got there, Joel finds Michael's hand in his, warm and pliant, like a sleeping puppy. The hand lets itself be shaken.

They all walk into the living room and sit. Artie is speaking. He has been speaking since the door opened. Lang is silent, occasionally smiles to himself.

The idea is simple. Up in Woodstock, New York, a colony of important rock stars has grown up: Dylan, Tim Hardin, the Band. What they need is a recording studio so they won't have to come to New York every time they want to cut an album. Artie isn't counting solely on local talent to provide business, however. He wants to build a retreat for rock musicians, a place where they can get away from everything, create, rap, Be: a haven with all New York's advantages and none of its hassles.

Joel and John listen. They are themselves in the process of building a large recording complex called Media Sound on West 57th Street. In that sense, they have "done" a studio already, and this is a negative factor. Also, despite themselves, despite Miles Lourie's injunction, the way Lang and Kornfeld look makes them uneasy. They are businessmen. These two . . . aren't, couldn't be. Not really.

Yet Kornfeld is surprisingly well-spoken, whether in absolute terms or only in terms of someone with his appearance is hard to judge. By any standards, he is smooth. There isn't a trace of pushiness in his delivery. He projects an air of disinterested conviction. He believes in his idea, he is committed to it, but he seems to keep it in perspective: it is not one of the vital things in his life, being merely a matter of money.

Kornfeld finishes his presentation. Lang gives him a congratulatory nod.

Joel and John look over the cost estimates and project outline together. As John is reluctantly about to decline to participate in the venture, something at the end of the outline sparks Joel's interest.

"Artie, what's this entry here about a press party?"

Kornfeld explains that their plans include an opening day concert for the under- and aboveground press, industry reps, investors, and so on. He thinks it likely that the local talent, once made to see that the recording studio/retreat is a valuable resource for them, will contribute their services or ask for only token remuneration. And this local talent, he reminds them, is not just any local talent.

"About how many people would you expect at this concert?" Joel asks.

"Four, five thousand," Artie answers.

Joel and John look at each other for a moment. Then John says, "Why don't you let the concert pay for the studio?"

"How do you mean?" Artie asks.

Joel replies, "Well, let's say that instead of a one-day concert for five thousand people, you have a two-day concert for, say, fifty thousand."

"And use the proceeds to build the studio?"

Joel and John nod yes.

"Well, now, that's a whole different project. . . ."

"It'd be a groove," Lang breaks in. The other three men turn to look at him. The face is in its impish mode, but the tone of voice is serious.

"A hundred thousand people in two days. Man, that would be heavy! Monterey didn't draw much over half of that."

Joel looks at John as if to say, "It talks!" "What do you think it would cost to put on a concert like that, Michael, including talent and everything?"

"Well, it would be expensive. Maybe $100,000 for talent, another hundred for expenses."

Artie quickly adds, "At five dollars a head each day, that leaves $300,000 profit."

Smiles light the room.

"Sounds interesting," says John.

"It's not what we had in mind though," Artie interjects. "And our share of $300,000 wouldn't pay for the construction of the studio."

"Well, look," suggests Joel, "why don't you two work up a proposal for the concert on paper. After we've seen that, maybe we can work out a deal for the studio based on it."

"O.K.," says Lang. "I like the idea."

"I do, too, at this point," John adds. "It sounds feasible,

and not really all that risky. After all, how much trouble can you get into putting on a concert?"

Joel on Friends and Family

Nobody was untouched by the Great Depression, and while my folks never stood on a bread line or had to go without a new pair of shoes, the economic tenor of those days transformed their mentality.

My father never sat me down and said in so many words, "Son, it's a cruel world out there and you better make sure you have a secure source of income before you do anything else," but I got the message anyway, watching him run several dental offices in at least three different locations on Long Island from seven o'clock in the morning until about the time I was supposed to be asleep.

My family wasn't wealthy, at least not as I understand wealth these days, but we were quite well off thanks to my father's heroic industriousness. Well before my sister, my brother, and I were old enough to hold down summer jobs, we were put to work around the house so that we could learn these patterns of industry, too. We got tiny allowances of twenty-five cents a week (U.S.) which we could augment only by making ourselves useful à la weeding the garden, shining shoes, cleaning out the garage, etc. We were taught, among other things, that using your noggin was always the preferred way of doing anything. "Don't force it," my father was fond of saying when a door was stuck or a jar wouldn't open.

The traditional stress on education for which Jewish families are notorious attained almost Scribal dimensions among us Rosenmans. Those in my parents' generation had gone to college, and many had gone on to graduate school as well, in the hopes of rising above the human condition. Lawyers and doctors hung from every branch of the family tree, and there was never much question about what sort of thing the son of one of Cold Spring Harbor's only dentists would end up doing. I don't mean to give the impression that my father tried to push me into oral hygiene. I think he mentioned it once in my life, and even then very tentatively. "Are you thinking at all of perhaps going into dentistry as your profession?" I was going into one profession or another, you see. The only question was which.

Summer employment came along to Build Character. For a while, Douglas and I free-lanced simonizing cars around the neighborhood. We did a good job, and the money was great. So great, in fact, that we decided to speed up production with a power buffer, a use of the noggin that backfired when, in a moment of inattention, I cut a ten-inch strip of paint off a highly conspicuous section of my uncle Jack's '52 Buick. Rosenman & Rosenman Simonizing quickly became Rosenman & Rosenman Lawn-mowing, and who knows what might have happened to the local greenswards had not Douglas and I landed a couple of cushy life-guarding jobs. I say cushy, but I was always so terrified that someone would disappear beneath the waves while I was on duty that I watched like a fanatic. All the suicidals went over to Fire Island as a result, and four years of vigilance passed without so much as an eyelash cramp in my bailiwick.

So then I went to Princeton, which was a real Mitzvah for the folks. How could a kid—especially a Jewish kid—go to a place like Princeton and not turn out to be somebody. A lawyer maybe, or even a doctor. But I started singing when I got to New Jersey; first in the glee club, then in a triple quartet, then in a trio, then some nightclub stuff. Before long I had plenty of money and a secret notion of where the action was in the business world. By the time I got to the end of my senior year, I felt I was at a crossroads. Rather than make a decision, I went, as I said, to Yale Law School.

From the outside, that looked like the beginning of a brilliant career in the legal profession. From the inside (of my grade sheet) it looked more and more like a singing career. I had some gigs in New York and landed a nightclub job at what at that time was *the* Holiday Inn in New Haven. Then came graduation, the New York Bar, the family firm, etc.

By the time that Grace and Bernie Rosenman learned that their son was planning a daring excursion into venture capital, it was somewhat after the fact. We had already placed our ads in the *Times* and the *Wall Street Journal* announcing our "unlimited capital" and that we were seeking "interesting, legitimate investment opportunities" to squander it on.* I had already been in touch with an edgy gentleman from Massachusetts who claimed to have the exclusive importation license for a device called the "skibob." Most important, I had already decided that the life I had been living did not remotely resemble the interstellar existence that now awaited me.

"It sounds like a lot of foolishness," said Bernie. "All this talk of deals and financing and getting into things firsthand. What you need is a solid base, a foundation. You don't start at the top and work upward. You build from something your own size to something bigger. . . ."

It didn't help any that I had been green enough to call our firm Challenge International, Limited, or that for the first eighteen months of our corporate life the deals I examined *ad nauseum* invariably ended up *ad museum*. I was eager as hell to get in on a deal; anything, just to get moving. But my natural instinct for avoiding what was obviously garbage enforced a kind of inactivity that seemed eternal.

Jock was of little help during this first year and a half. Pathetically, he looked to me for leadership, since, by an accident of genetics, I had grown up to be stronger, smarter, more energetic, and more imaginative than he was. First thing each morning I had to soothe his anxiety by telling him that all was not permanently frozen into stagnation. The rest of the day had to be spent dissuading him from plunging into some cockamamie scheme that his adorable but imperfectly balanced intellect had hatched over lunch.

As the months of inactivity dragged on, I began to notice that my law-school mates were moving ahead in a slow but secure way within their law firms. It occurred to me that I would never be able to support and raise a family if I kept sitting

New York Times, March 22, 1967, p. 54: "Young men with unlimited capital looking for interesting, legitimate investment opportunities and business propositions."

around all the time waiting for something to happen But we kept plugging away at nothing until finally one day, to the immense relief of all concerned, we got into the Media Sound project. It involved building a recording studio from the ground up, and we were thrilled to be part of it. It wasn't the greatest deal in the world, but, coming when it did, it was a godsend.

To the outside observer, namely, Bernie, Media Sound looked like good business experience—the kind that prepares you for bigger things. It still puzzles him that I went *from* Media Sound *to* Woodstock.

John on Friends and Family

I don't know who we'll end up dedicating this book to if we ever get it published, but if there's any justice in the world, the honor should go to my family. They suffered more and died more horrible deaths than anyone outside of Joel and myself—and all without chance of reward. In addition, when things got really heavy and all of their dire predictions were exceeded tenfold by reality, they dropped everything and rallied to our aid. Our problems became their problems and, even to this day, not one of them has exercised his perfectly legitimate option of saying, "I told you so, you dumb-ass."

After the Festival, some uncharacteristically accurate newspaper stories were printed about how lucky I was to have such understanding and generous relatives. My father and my brothers issued noble-sounding statements to the effect that the Roberts clan had never been associated with bankruptcy in the past and wasn't going to start now. My father even went so far as to utter for publication, "John is a good boy. He's bright and hard-working. He'll do all right." Corny, right? Old-fashioned? Maybe so, but for my money—what's left of it—my family showed a lot of class, and the love I've always felt for them was augmented by a heaping dollop of respect.

Prior to the Festival, however, intrafamily relations weren't all that smooth. My father, you see, is a pessimist. He fervently *hopes* that good things will happen, but he *knows* better and arms himself against the crashes yet to come. Example:—Me: "Hi, Dad. I'm just calling to say good-by. I'm off to Vegas for the weekend." Him: "Try not to lose more than five thousand." Example:—Me: "Hi, Dad. We just bought an apartment. I think we got a good deal." Him: "It would have cost you less if you'd waited a year." Example:—Me: "Hi, Dad. I bought this great new stock yesterday." Him: "How much is it down?" Et cetera.

My brother Billy is a different type altogether: the family optimist. Though shrewd, *e.g.*, he didn't get involved in Woodstock, he is a firm believer in the power of positive thinking, *e.g.*, "Woodstock's a winner." Along with my father, he has an excellent sense of humor, although up till now the three of us have shared remarkably few belly laughs over the Festival.

My other brother, Keith, is the family revolutionary. Disdaining business as the last refuge of lazy scoundrels, he has pursued a career in the law and public service. He rallied round during our time *in extremis*, mustering his considerable talent for indignation. He felt that Joel and I had been out-lazy-scoundreled by our partners, and he introduced me accordingly to his good friend William Kunstler, the attorney. This led me to make one of my few winning decisions of the year. I turned down Bill Kunstler's services. I don't mean to belittle Keith's efforts by saying that either. He was instrumental in solving some thorny legal problems, and he rendered yeoman service in raising the dough to pay off our creditors. We owe him a great deal. Not cash, thank God.

But, as I was saying, relations within the family were not smooth. My father's pessimism, being ideally suited to a project with Woodstock's potential, soon turned that gentle soul into a veritable prophet of doom. He grew more and more annoyed that I was sinking more and more money into the Festival fiasco, and I grew more and more annoyed that he was growing more and more annoyed and not crediting me with an ounce of good sense. Meanwhile, Billy's wholehearted verbal support of the undertaking was clashing with his equally wholehearted fiscal nonparticipation, and the conflict didn't help our rapport one bit. Keith, finally, seemed to take the attitude that the whole enterprise constituted the crassest sort of exploitation, and that, of course, endeared him to me no end.

My friends were better disposed. They looked on Woodstock as a normal outgrowth of the John Roberts they had known and liked. I was considered somewhat eccentric, somewhat imaginative, and somewhat wealthy. Ergo . . . Woodstock. Some of them, I believe, took a certain vicarious pride in all the publicity I got, but that was balanced off by the fact that they all had parents who used me as an example of what happens to young men who have too much too soon.

The only real *tsouris* I got from my friends was the constant question: "What are you gonna do about people taking a dump?" I would explain that we had two thousand toilets on order from Johnny-on-the-Spot. "But how are the trucks gonna get through to empty the cans?" they would counter. My stock answer after a while was: "We're gonna hand out bananas at the gates to bind our patrons."

Of course, at that time I didn't know there weren't going to be any gates.

A Restaurant Scene

A Small Midtown Restaurant on Madison Avenue
Tuesday, March 18, 1969, 1:30 P.M.

John Roberts is sitting at a table with his father, his eldest brother, Billy, and his father's wife, Marjorie. They have just come from the funeral of John's uncle, and the general mood around the table is subdued. The main course is eaten in silence. Over coffee a desultory conversation begins during which one gets the impression that Mr. Roberts is testing the ground in the vicinity of a particular subject while John is preparing himself for an imminent battle of wills.

"Well," says Mr. Roberts, "so the Media Sound project is pretty well under way."

"Yes, Dad," John answers. "Things are moving right along."

Billy Roberts, who has always regarded John with big-brotherly condescension, glances from father to son with an amused glint in his eye. Mrs. Roberts, having not yet detected any ominous vibrations, quietly sips her coffee.

"So," says Mr. Roberts, "now you just keep tabs on it, right? Start making your investment back?"

John shifts uneasily in his chair. "I guess so, Dad. Yeah. That's pretty much it."

"I see."

Silence again falls on the table. Billy grins mischievously as his glowering father takes a bite out of his coffee. John tries to look casual, as though the tension in the air, which now even Mrs. Roberts has noticed, did not exist.

After a few minutes, Mr. Roberts speaks again. "That'll keep you busy, will it? Keeping tabs on things."

"Well, no, Dad," says John, laughing nervously. "Not really."

"No, eh?" Mr. Roberts murmurs. "Well then, what else are you doing?"

John clears his throat. "Actually, Dad, something very interesting has come up."

Mr. Roberts' eyes narrow. "Oh?"

"Yes. We, uh, we've formed a corporation with two other guys."

"A corporation, eh," says Mr. Roberts, pausing for effect. "To do what?"

"Well, we've decided to put on this really huge concert. This August. Have over a hundred thousand people."

"You're going to put on a concert?"

"That's what we're planning, Dad."

"A . . . a concert?"

John nods.

"Where?"

"A town up north of Poughkeepsie called Woodstock."

"You're going to put on a concert for a hundred thousand people in a town?"

"No. Well, yes. I mean, not in the town itself. Outside the

town. In Saugerties. On some land we're checking on at the moment."

"Let me understand this. You're going to put on a concert in some field a hundred miles from New York."

"Well, yes. I guess that's what it amounts to."

"What's wrong with a field twenty miles from New York?"

"Oh, sorry. I should have mentioned, this place Woodstock is sort of a gathering place for singers, musicians, composers, people like that. It's very well known."

"So is Tanglewood. You have a better attraction than the Boston Symphony?"

"The Boston . . . ? Oh! Sorry again. My mistake. All those singers and musicians in Woodstock are rock stars. We're putting on a rock concert."

"A rock concert! How exciting!" says Mrs. Roberts, drawing an angry growl from her husband which goes unnoticed. "It sounds like a fabulous idea. Is there any stock or things for sale?"

"Marjorie!" Mr. Roberts explodes.

"What's wrong, Alfred?"

"The whole project is harebrained. That's what's wrong. Billy, are you in on this?"

Billy leans back happily in his chair. "Well, I know about it, Dad. But I think I'll let the boys handle this one on their own. Should be great experience for them. They'll learn a lot, get their feet wet, maybe make a little money even."

"Oh yes, money," Alfred Roberts says. "What's the bankroll on this project?"

John glares at Billy for a moment and then looks at his father. "Two hundred and fifty thousand."

"Aargh," says Mr. Roberts, slapping his forehead.

"Now, Dad, it may sound like a lot, but when you consider that maybe an average of forty thousand people are going to pay six or seven dollars for tickets each day . . ."

"Each day! What each day?"

"Well, we're planning on having this concert over the course of three days, a weekend."

"Three days? In a field? What if it rains?"

"Listen, Dad, we've started going into all those kinds of details. I mean, this thing is going to take a lot of planning. But we're getting the best people we can and we've got six months to get ready."

"For what? Bankruptcy?"

"Dad!"

"Well, I'm sorry, Jock. But the whole thing is preposterous. Even if you do make all the right preparations, what on earth makes you think that a hundred thousand people—a hundred thousand—are going to be stupid enough to drive a hundred miles to listen to rock music? Why, you have concerts right here in New York that don't draw one tenth of that."

John looks at his father dejectedly. "I don't know what to tell you, Dad. We may not draw a hundred thousand. I don't know. But Joel and I wouldn't have gotten involved in this if we hadn't considered all the angles. Even if we only draw fifty thousand, we'll still make our expenses back."

"Fifty thousand," Alfred Roberts says, shaking his head. "You'll be lucky if a hundred people show up."

PARTNERS

Joel on Diesel

Diesel was a down and dirty rock group that began rolling along the tracks on a collision course with Woodstock Ventures—the name we gave our concert corporation—several months before Michael and Artie entered my life. In fact, it was Diesel that brought Michael and Artie together. Of course, I wasn't present at that momentous first encounter, so I can only speculate on what took place. In the light of subsequent developments, however, the following account can be taken as a reasonable reconstruction.

Artie, the head of Contemporary Product, is seated in his office at Capitol when in walks Michael bearing new-mown tobacco. Cigarettes are immediately rolled and ignited, and after both men level off at cruising altitude, Michael reveals that he is the personal manager of a new group that Artie has got to hear.

Enter Diesel, behaired and begrimed in the best acid-rock tradition, complete with buckskin jackets, cowboy boots, aged blue jeans, thick leather belts with elaborate handmade buckles, and one or two funky hats with floppy brims for the flies to light on when they get tired of hovering.

Michael breaks out some demonstration tapes, and, scant minutes later, Artie is on the phone to his boss, Alan Livingstone, to inform him that he has discovered the group of the year. Livingstone, trusting Artie's judgment in these matters, says to sign 'em up, and when Artie puts down the phone the room fills with grunts of "Groovy," "Far out," "Heavy," "Outta sight," and other approximations of satisfaction.

More tobacco is trotted out, and even Diesel smokes. Not that they are abstemious by nature, but their drug of choice tends to be alcohol; and chronic. Right now, though, if the five dollars they need for their next fifth of Four Roses is to be made secure, they must play along with these two shitbird hippies whom, if the truth were known, they would just as soon pound into a permanent coma as look at.

So much for the history of the thing. Once Michael and Artie insinuated themselves into Woodstock, it was only a matter of time until primal instincts such as fear and greed impelled them to bring their collection of prerecidivists into the corporate bosom along with them. For a while they laid the groundwork with occasional reverent allusions to their protégés, and then they sprang their proposal that Diesel become a property of our management arm, Woodstock Kalaparusha.

Their reasoning went as follows: one could make a lot of money by developing and breaking a good rock act; Diesel was a good rock act; develop Diesel and break it at the Festival, in style. I mumbled something to the effect that the whole thing seemed like a diversion from our main objectives, but Artie didn't get to drive gold Corvettes on an expense account by being unprepared for such objections.

"Hey, man, like I gotta tell ya, Diesel is our gig. Before Woodstock even, man. We can't just split from them. It wouldn't be right." Or safe. "Like, dig it: they're our home and Woodstock is our home, and you can't live in two homes at once. So let's ask 'em to move in with us so we'll all be pulling together for the same things."

I admit that the warmth of this appeal really touched me. Here were my new partners concerned not only for the grubbiest of their former obligations, but anxious to preclude even the shadow of a conflict of interest with their new ones. I temporized some more, but my heart wasn't in it, and before long we had signed a contract guaranteeing our support of Diesel forever and bestowing a hefty reimbursement of expenses and a commission on our own Michael Lang.

It bothers me even now that I could have been such a cow plop. It wasn't as though I hadn't heard the group play. I had. But all I concluded from their sound was that I was missing the nuances. I had permitted myself to be maneuvered into believing that Michael and Artie were apostles of a new awareness who saw and heard things too finely pitched for my blunt sensors. In fact, they saw and heard dollar signs and cash-register clangs backed up by the threat of a severe stomping if they didn't deliver in accordance with Diesel's expectations.

The element of fear in Michael's and Artie's machinations was something else that totally eluded me in those euphoric days. I remember one incident, which should have been particularly illuminating and wasn't, in which a dispute arose as to which of them would attend a Diesel rehearsal over at Capitol. Neither wanted to sit in on the session because the group was growing suspicious of their assurances that an actual recording session was imminent, and a suspicious Diesel was likely to jump its tracks and come after you.

Anyone less eager than I was at the time would have detected the uncharacteristic strain in Artie's voice as he said, "Hey, like it's your turn, man. Dig it?" and in Michael's when he replied, "Hey, man, like it isn't." But no amount of eagerness can excuse my missing the significance of the manner in which the dispute was resolved. What happened was that Artie broke out a roll of hundreds and peeled one off for Michael, who took it without enthusiasm. I chose to interpret this bit of business as a mutual triumph of amiable self-indulgence and intelligent self-interest. The possibility that Artie's cowardice was greater than his avarice while Michael's avarice was greater than his cowardice did not occur to me.

My perceptions were so distorted that it took Diesel itself to clear them up. They accomplished this during their first paid booking under our sponsorship by engaging the bouncer at the Electric Circus in a kneeish knuckly discussion about the propriety of their having thrown an electric bass guitar through the establishment's enormous plate-glass front window. The bouncer apparently identified with electric bass guitars and prevailed upon each of Diesel to follow its path through what was left of the window so that they, too, could understand the nature of its trajectory. It was a fitting end to the whole episode and uncomfortably symbolic of Woodstock's future investments: money out the window.

John on Stock Tips for Mike and Artie

My father-in-law has an expression he uses whenever someone offers a pie-in-the-sky proposition: "He who believes it becomes holy." Translation: "You're either a saint or an idiot, and I'm betting on the latter." Perhaps that's why my broker refers to me as St. Jocko the Stupid. But there was a time back in the late sixties when I was hot in the Market. I had a string of two winners at one point, and the fact that two chimpanzees selecting stocks at random would have made enough in those days to open their own investment firm—I know several who did, come to think of it—didn't prevent me from strutting around flexing my genius. Thus Michael and Artie came to think of me as Woodstock's "financial cat," and approached me one early spring day with one of their rattiest schemes of exploitation.

"Hey, man," said Artie, "ya got any hot tips in the Market? I mean, like Woodstock oughta have an investment wing, ya dig? Like, I gotta tell ya, we oughta diversify. We're heavy in the music business, and we gotta let the bread work for us in the Market, too."

"Far out!" seconded Michael, tittering. "We gotta have a . . . a . . . portfolio."

He and Artie then tittered *a cappella* and gave each other five, joyful at the prospect of imminent capital gains.

Not one to dampen such enthusiasm, I allowed as how I just might have a couple of items of interest. But it would be sheer folly to invest corporately, I cautioned. Far better to do it individually; for tax considerations, of course.

Of course, they agreed, none of us understanding why.

"But I don't have all that much money," said Artie, never behindhand in substituting blatant hints when subtle ones are ignored.

"Start small," I advised him, never behindhand in deftly parrying attempted touches. "In this market, you'll build up a big capital base in no time."

Artie started to protest, but I moved to put the lid on it. "I definitely don't think corporate investment is a proper activity for Woodstock at this juncture. We're fully budgeted for the currently proposed activities, after all. And then, of course, Diesel . . ."

The unspoken rebuke dangled meaningfully in the air, and off in a corner, the darkling Joel heaved an audible sigh of relief.

"All right, man," said Artie, quick to regroup, "lay some tips on us."

"Right," I said. "Now here's a little stock . . ." and I proceeded to weave a web of simulated profits that positively made them drool. Joel fell asleep, he and I having invested in the same little number some months ago. It had enjoyed a tiny surge and then subsided into the dogdrums, where it was currently becalmed. If the Wandering Jew could be made to lie down with the Sheik of Araby, this stock had a chance. Otherwise it was beetling toward an early insolvency.

I still don't know what got into me that day. Maybe even then I had a premonition about those two. Perhaps I just resented their rapaciously pushy efforts to use my money to buy themselves stock. Whatever it was, I laid a bummer on them that afternoon that they didn't soon forget, and at the end of my glowing analysis they raced to the phone to call a cousin or somebody and bought as much of the beast as margin would allow.

In moments of extreme paranoia, *i.e.*, weekdays and alternate Sundays, I believe that the stocks I run across by chance are, in reality, sentient organisms capable of considerable malevolence. They all have the same mission: to make up attractive stories about themselves, see to it that John Roberts of New York City gets wind of them, descend like an express elevator at the Empire State Building as soon as he buys, hover briefly at the fiftieth floor and then rise a story or two to get him to double up on his holding, and, lastly, plummet to the basement as if the cables had snapped. The stock I gave Michael and Artie didn't have that big a trip to make. It was approaching the lobby when they bought it at nine and it disappeared into the subsoil about four months later. Joel and I eked out a modest profit by exiting on a hunch at seven and a quarter. Michael and Artie got out a little later; seven points later, to be precise. Oddly enough, they never mentioned the Woodstock investment wing again, but I don't think they forgot about it either.

On August 14, I was at the site with Michael, surveying the $200,000 pile of wood and wire that was supposed to have been a stage for the world's greatest rock performers. I was wondering why none of the wood and wire seemed to go together and how the hell they could be made to in the space of one day. Michael was wondering something else.

"Hey, John," he said, "that stock you told me to buy is out of action. What do you think I should do?"

Was he gloating about some horrible revenge he was about to exact? Was he needling me about my bad judgment in the Market? Or was he, in the midst of chaos, simply passing the time of day? It is a measure of Michael that, to this day, I still can't do more than just hazard a guess.

An Evening at the Kornfelds

36th Floor, 400 East 56th Street, Manhattan
Saturday, March 22, 1969, 10:15 P.M.

Artie Kornfeld's apartment is bathed in a dim orange light which radiates in diffuse beams from several fixtures on the ceiling. A deep-pile wall-to-wall carpet covers the floor, as do roughly half a dozen bodies, among which Joel's and John's can be discerned. Artie is draped across one of the two immense overstuffed armchairs in the room. His wife sits at his feet, gazing pensively off into space at a thirty-degree downward angle. The voice of Bob Dylan comes from the impressive stereo rig. Michael Lang, his face at its most oxymoronic, is sitting on the floor opposite Artie. He is smiling with such concentrated beatitude that one cannot help attributing to him an almost supernatural capacity for evil. The odor of smoke is everywhere, covering the air like a hot fudge blanket.

The doorbell rings, and John, still a bit uneasy in these surroundings, snaps himself off the floor into an alert seated position.

"That must be the cat with the Chinese food," says Artie as he glides toward the door, wallet at the ready.

He returns with an enormous brown paper bag, which he takes to the table and begins to empty. The smell of food pierces the smoky overlay.

With that peculiar susceptibility to appetite so common to chain smokers, all the formerly inert figures on the floor swim into close orbits around the table. They serve themselves, and the room fills with muted rumbles of olfactory and gustatory satisfaction.

Into the midst of this low-key feeding frenzy crawls a small child. Kornfeld puts down his plate and goes over to her. She looks up at him with big inquiring eyes.

"Hello, Jamie, honey," he says as he bends to pick her up. Then, to Joel's amusement and John's disgust, he unlooses a torrent of baby talk. After fully venting his affection, he carries the child over to his wife. "You want to hold her for a while, Linda?" She answers with a glowing maternal smile which, quite apart from being lovely to contemplate in its own right, puts the recent spate of paternal mush into its proper perspective. Artie hands her the infant and beams happily down at the tableau that results. He then picks up his plate and joins Joel and John on the floor near where Michael is seated.

"Man, this stuff is out of sight. Out . . . of . . . sight!"

"You mean the Chinese food or the, uh, vegetables?" Joel asks.

Artie laughs. "Both, man. Both."

From across the room, one of Artie's friends inquires about the health of a well-known rock singer-composer.

"He's O.K.," Artie responds. "I think he just ran into some bad dope. It was a bummer, man. I mean, one day he's telling me about this gig he's got to play in fucking Tucson—that's the way he said it, 'fucking Tucson,' like Greater Minneapolis—and then I hear he's in the Tucson hospital."

"Don't any of those people ever worry about going to jail?" John asks.

"Well, it doesn't pay to sweat a bust, man. Life's too short. Besides, I don't think I know two people who ever got busted. Anybody here ever get busted? Freddie? Paul? . . . Jamie?"

Everyone laughs, and Jamie, sensing that she has become the center of attention, laughs, too, and gurgles. Her mother's smile takes on additional luster.

"I've never been busted, but I've come pretty close," says Michael quietly, without elaborating.

"How do you mean, Michael? What happened?" Joel asks.

Michael intensifies his smile and his face turns startlingly Mephistophelian in the orange light. He is Rosemary's baby at twenty-four, or Rosemary's baby's father.

"Come on, man," Artie coaxes.

"Well, one time I was going up to see a friend. And I couldn't get in the door."

Everyone looks at him expectantly. After a considerable interval, John says, "And . . . ?"

"And, that's it," says Michael. "Like, my friend was in the process of being busted at the time."

"And the door was locked?" asks John. "It wouldn't open?"

"No, man. The door wasn't locked. It was just that I couldn't open it."

Joel frowns in concentration. "Michael, you mean that the . . . vibes coming from inside stopped you. Actually prevented you?"

"Yeah," says Michael matter-of-factly.

Joel and John look at each other, at Michael, around the room, and at each other again.

"But that's impossible," John wails. "Anybody can open . . ."

"It's not impossible, man," Michael stated gently and softly.

"That's really strange," Joel murmurs after awhile.

"What's strange?" Michael asks.

"The idea of being physically incapacitated by vibes. Weird."

Artie breaks in with a laugh, "It's weirder when you don't feel any vibrations at all, man. That's why the world is so fucked up. It's full of weird people who don't feel anything. Michael's the only normal cat around."

This brings general laughter and approval.

Joel and John feel considerably out of their depth. It is not the first time since they met Michael and Artie.

MAKING WALLKILL

A Legal Interlude

An Attorney's Office on Park Avenue in the Mid-eighties
Tuesday, March 25, 1969, 11:00 A.M.

Joel and John, after just under an hour's wait, have been ushered into the inner office and are seated facing the attorney. He looks at them with an air of mild distaste. They look at him with expressions of unconcealed exasperation.

"I understand from Mr. Lang that you are interested in leasing some of my client's acreage in Saugerties."

John replies, "We understand from Mr. Lang that negotiations have proceeded somewhat further than an expression of interest."

"Mr. Lang, I take it, is your associate."

Joel and John nod.

"And you gentlemen represent . . ." Here there is a long pause as the attorney sifts casually through the papers on his desk. "Ah, here we are. You represent this, uh, corporation called Challenge International, Limited. Is that correct?"

Joel and John nod again, lips tight.

"You are engaged in investment banking?"

"Venture capital," Joel says.

"Ah, venture capital." He sifts through his papers again. "You would be Mr. Roberts?" he enquires of Joel.

"Mr. Rosenman."

"Ah, Mr. Rosenman. I see from your financial statement that you have a car."

Joel stares at him in disbelief. "Yes."

"Is it financed?"

"I beg your pardon?"

"Is it financed?"

"Excuse me," John breaks in, "but we came here to discuss your client's land."

"You would be Mr. Roberts?"

"I would."

"I'm delighted to see that you enjoy a very favorable financial position, judging by this figure for your net worth. I'm afraid that I don't find an itemized list of your assets here though."

"No," John agrees, "you don't."

"I shall require one."

Joel heads off an epithet from his partner by saying, "Look, Mr. Lang told us that your client . . ."

"Ah, Mr. Lang. Yes. From what I see here, Mr. Lang is devoid of assets. I pray that his weekly wage is adequate for his maintenance."

No one says amen.

"And Mr. Kornfeld. He lists here a one-acre beachfront property. Where would that be?"

"That would be on Eleuthera," says John. "Now about this lease."

"Just so. Mr. Lang and Mr. Kornfeld would be prepared to add their personal guarantees to this agreement of lease you have in mind?"

"We're prepared to make all appropriate guarantees," John replies. "But it would be helpful to know how much your client wants in the way of rent, the amount of acreage available, et cetera."

"Quite. For what purpose do you desire the use of the land?"

"As we said in our letter," Joel answers, "we want to put on a three-day music festival."

"Ah, yes. A music festival. I see that Mr. Kornfeld does not state the make of his car. He describes it as, quote, a sixty-nine convertible, unquote."

"It's a Corvette." John sighs wearily. "A gold Corvette."

The attorney notes this on a spotless pad of yellow legal paper.

"Fine. Now then, do you have any basis for assuming that my client is prepared to lease this land to you?"

Joel and John look at each other and then at the attorney. "Mr. Lang informed us that he is," Joel says.

"Ah, Mr. Lang," says the attorney, chuckling complacently to himself. "I must tell you that my client wishes to keep this land inviolate for his sons. As far as I know, he has no intention of renting it for any purposes whatsoever." He sits up proudly in his chair. "He is a man of means."

"Well, perhaps if you could contact him . . ." John says weakly.

"Yes, of course. First, though, I shall require more information than I have thus far been furnished with. By whom, for example, was Mr. Kornfeld employed prior to his obtaining his current position with Capitol Records?"

Walking back to their apartment a few minutes later, Joel and John say little. The feeling that things are not proceeding smoothly needs no articulation.

John on the Mills Property

Howard Mills was a man who owned some six hundred acres of land in Wallkill, New York, which he wanted to turn into an industrial park. He may have succeeded. I don't know. I don't even care. Like most things associated with Woodstock, I try not to think about it very much.

As the reader has already learned, the Saugerties property that, according to Michael and Artie, had already "gone down," went up in smoke before we ever set foot on it. Consequently, it behooved our new corporate body to find another site pronto, lest we commit the crime of trespass by festival. We toyed briefly with ads that read:

SNEAK UP ON THE POCANTICO HILLS
FOR THREE DAYS OF PEACE AND MUSIC
AND HELP LIBERATE THE NORTH FORTY

But the concept didn't wash. Then, toward the end of March, Joel and I took matters into our own hands. As was our custom, we decided to act boldly, *i.e.*, without proper thought.

On Sunday, March 30, I woke up to the sound of the Byrds, a group I have always detested. I realized at once that I had forgotten to turn off my radio the night before. As I reached over to silence the offending device, Joel came into my room and said, "Let's take the car and go upstate to look for some land."

A scant few hours later, I found myself racing merrily along the Major Deegan Expressway while Joel and the car sat stationary, waiting for me to return with a bucket of gasoline. By noon, the problem had been solved, and we were on our way.

The general object of the day's exercise was to find real-estate brokers in remote rural areas and ask them if there were any large parcels of land, say six hundred acres, that we could rent for the summer. After several near misses—"No, we don't deal in acreage as large as that, but I can rent you a nice forty-foot lakefront"—we happened upon an agency that specialized in industrial parks. An industrial park is not a place where blast furnaces go to roller-skate. It is land that has been zoned for industrial development. It is usually large and ugly and empty. Then industry arrives and it is no longer empty.

I have forgotten the name of the realtor who put us on to the Mills land, which is probably a good thing for both of us. Whoever he was, he told us that he had just what we were looking for over Middletown way, Middletown being the town in which the township of Wallkill was located, or vice versa. It cost us a pretty penny not to figure that out, by the way, because we were sued later by the real town (township) of Wallkill, somewhere up in the Adirondacks or the Poconos or the Urals, for using its name in our ads when what we really meant was the township (town) of Wallkill right there in Ulster County.

Make that Orange County.

The real-estate agent called a man named Howard Mills and asked him if he would be interested in leasing out his land for the summer. He was. He told us to come straight over and tell him what it was all about, so we hopped back into the car and headed off to see him, stopping once so that Joel could be at the wheel when the mileage indicator read exactly ten thousand.

We all have our quirks.

Several hundred miles beyond the county line we began to suspect that we had missed the proper turnoff. Reacting swiftly to signs announcing the approach of the Canadian border, we turned around and managed to arrive back in Wallkill toward dusk. We asked a traffic cop for directions to the Mills Industrial Park, and he pointed ominously to some barren hilly land in front of us and said that was it. There was a small paved road leading in, and we followed it for several hundred yards. It rose gradually, dominated by a hideous green water tower and flanked by fallow fields. Part of the acreage had been plowed, and in those areas the unappetizing redness of the soil base stood revealed. About fifty acres were given over to apple trees, but, save for a small house situated at the end of the road, the rest of the property was empty. This was the Mills home, and pacing back and forth outside it was Mills.

After some testy questions and evasive answers about our tardiness, we settled down to talk turkey. Several gobbles later, Mills had been made to understand that we wanted his land for a music and art fair in August. We would need to do some developing, bulldoze some roads, clear some trees, build a stage, and erect fences, but by August 20 or so the land would be restored to him in its original condition. Mills said that sounded fine. All we had to do was get approval from the local Zoning Board. If that was forthcoming, why for $10,000 we were welcome to the use of his property.

At this point our only problem was that we weren't sure our partners would approve, but we saw no reason not to take an option. We finally agreed with Mills that, pending approval by the Zoning Board and Michael and Artie, we would take a thirty-day two-way option for $1,500. Either party could refuse to exercise it: us, if the land wasn't suitable; him, if we weren't. He said his lawyer would work up the papers and send them to us in New York.

Flushed with triumph, Joel and I returned to the city. For the first time, we felt that the project was really under way. We had done something concrete, and as soon as we got in, we called Michael to tell him about it all. "It's nothing fantastic," we said, "but it's land. Actual contiguous acres!" Michael was dubious about the vibes of an industrial park, but he agreed to go up with his land experts the next day and have a look.

Go up he did—in a helicopter—and after a long and costly survey, the land was pronounced . . . adequate. Barring some sort of calamity, we were in business.

The Wallkill Zoning Board of Appeals

The Town Hall, Wallkill, New York
Friday, April 18, 1969, 4:00 P.M.

In a moderately large room three men are seated at a table facing about a dozen rows of folding chairs, almost all of them empty. Near the center of the second row, Joel and John sit talking to their attorney. They are immaculately dressed—ties and business suits—and they behave as though they had just completed a cram course in deference. Their desire to give the impression that they are timid and unassuming infuses their every movement, and since no one really knows them here, the illusion is sustained. Michael and Artie are nowhere to be seen.

The man in the center seat at the table/dais is speaking to a thin, angry-looking woman in curlers. "Now look, Agnes. You know perfectly well that that trailer has no business being where it is. The ordinance is absolutely clear about this sort of thing, and if we made an exception for you, we'd have to make an exception for everybody."

"You made an exception for Ed Murphy. He kept his truck down there for three months and . . ."

"A truck's not a trailer, Agnes. You've got to move it."

"Oh crud!" says the woman, and stomps out.

The chairman sighs, sifts through some papers, and looks out toward the rows of chairs. "George," he says to Woodstock's attorney, "you want to go ahead now?"

The attorney stands. "Yes, thanks. I'd like to introduce Mr. Roberts and Mr. Rosenman, who're interested in putting on a little festival here this summer."

"Oh," says the chairman, "this is that thing about Howard Mills' property, right?"

"Right," George answers.

"Howard mentioned it to me when I saw him over at the shopping center the other day."

"Good. Then I'll just say that Mr. Roberts and Mr. Rosenman represent a promotional corporation in New York City called Woodstock Ventures, and they plan to put on a two-day music and art and drama festival on Howard's property. They would like to get the board's approval for the project and also want to let you know their plans so they can be sure that the zoning ordinance permits the sorts of things they have in mind."

The heavy man on the chairman's left yawns extravagantly.

"Thank you, George," says the chairman. "Would you have your clients tell us what they think will be involved."

The attorney turns and motions to John. "Mr. Roberts."

John rises. "Thank you. We're planning basically to put on a sort of fair, with top-flight musicians and art exhibits."

"What sort of art?" asks the heavy man.

"Well, amateur art mostly. I mean we're planning to have struggling young painters, ghetto artists, show their paintings, and then we'll give scholarships to the most promising."

"How many people you figure you'll have?" asks the third member of the board, a tiny man with a tremulous voice.

"Well, there's never been more than thirty or so thousand at an event of this kind, but we're hoping we might get lucky and have forty or even fifty thousand. I doubt that we will, though."

"You gonna have to do any building?" asks the chairman.

"Nothing permanent, sir. Maybe a tent to protect the paintings."

The heavy man suddenly stirs. "Did you say thirty or forty thousand people?"

"Well, yes. Spread over a couple of days, of course. If we're that fortunate."

The chairman frowns for a moment. "Well, if you're going to have anything like that many people, you are going to have to do some construction."

"Yessir, I suppose that's true."

"Well, what happens if someone gets hurt?"

The attorney stands up. "The lease my clients are going to enter into with Howard Mills provides for full liability insurance. But we're talking about totally private land, and I don't see how the town could be liable in any case."

"O.K.," says the chairman. "I just want to make sure that these kinds of things are being taken care of."

The attorney smiles. "Well, I think I can say pretty safely that there are going to be full preparations and that everything will be handled in a smooth and orderly manner. As I said, Mr. Roberts and Mr. Rosenman simply want to be certain they're in compliance with the statute and get your O.K."

The chairman glances to his right and his left. "Ed? Bill?" His colleagues make no sign. "Well, I guess there's no problem. Pending these boys getting their insurance, we'll say that the Zoning Board has no objections to what they're planning."

"Thank you very much," says Joel. "I just want to add that we hope the people of Wallkill will participate in and enjoy the Festival with us. I mean, we hope Wallkill with think of the Festival as a local cultural event, and enjoy the music and the art along with the visitors from other places."

The heavy man shifts in his chair. "Say, son, what kind of music you going to be putting on up here?"

"Well," says Joel, looking for help to John and the attorney, "I guess the best way to describe it would be, uh, folk. Basically folk. A little swing, too, maybe. A little jazz. You know."

The heavy man grunts. "This is a small town here, son. You know what I mean? We don't want anybody's feathers getting ruffled."

"Neither do we, sir," replies Joel with his most ingratiating smile. "After all, Wallkill's going to be like our home while we're up here."

The chairman leans back on his chair and stretches. "Well, everything seems O.K. to me. Anybody have any more questions they want to ask?"

There is silence.

"Good. Then the meeting's adjourned."

There will be other meetings, however.

PROGRESS (?) REPORT: APRIL 15

LAND: None

STAFF: Two secretaries

TICKET RECEIPTS: None

TALENT BOOKINGS: None

ATTORNEYS: One in New York City; one in Wallkill

PORTABLE TOILETS: None

MONEY SPENT: $57,000

IN BUSINESS

John on the Bank—I

I would like to deal swiftly with the painful matter of how we financed the Woodstock Festival.

In 1966, as I said, I came into a considerable amount of money, most of which I spent at once. The remainder I invested in the common stock of such Wall Street legends as Nosedive Industries and Consolidated Plunge, netting myself a nifty tax loss to carry forward into less bearish years. Had this money represented the bulk of my inheritance, I would have viewed its sudden disappearance with alarm, but my parents had wisely decided many years before that a lad of twenty-one was simply not capable of handling too much legal tender all in one lump. Accordingly, they had set up a trust and specified that no portion of the principal could be touched until my twenty-fifth birthday (in 1970). Even then, only a third of the total was to come into my hands. I would receive the second third when I was thirty and the final third when I was thirty-five. The trust income, however, was to be mine at age twenty-one, and it was this accumulated interest that I diddled away so rapidly in 1966.

It should come as no surprise that by 1967 the possibility of circumventing the provisions of the trust had become one of my major preoccupations. Joel and I had a number of potential business ventures that were in urgent need of money, and it seemed ridiculous to have all my lucre socked away just earning interest when it could have been out working as collateral.

Fortunately, nobody paid any attention to my whining for two full years, and many sure-fire business propositions, such as flying cars and power sources from the eighth dimension, went begging as a result. My trusts were inviolate, at least until the early part of 1969. Then my brother Billy began to see things my way. This made a big difference. First of all, he was older and, presumably, wiser. Secondly, he was considerably glibber. Thirdly, and most important, his money was tied up in trusts, too, and he had just met an elderly banker who knew how to cut it loose.

This kindly old gentleman worked for a bank that was and still is one of New York's major financial institutions, fast growing and profitable. It had an imaginative and intelligent lending policy. Unlike many other larger banks, this particular bank based its loans on the character and integrity of the borrower and not simply on his ability to repay. This latter was, of course, important. Banks, after all, do not lend on speculation as a matter of policy. But loans are made to people who can and sometimes do dishonor paper contracts. So their policy was, simply stated: Good people make for good loans. This policy was put to the test a little later on in the story.

Anyway, our banker friend invited my brother and me down to his bank one February morning and outlined a deal that would provide us with a gigantic line of credit in exchange for personal guarantees and a lien against our trusts. The understanding was that when the trusts terminated we would assign them to the Bank as straight collateral against any loans outstanding at the time. We jumped at the idea. Quite apart from the fact that it allowed us to circumvent the time-release provisions of the trust instruments, it enabled us to make any deals we wanted without having to go to some bank each time and haggle about financing.

Within a month of that morning, I met Lang and Kornfeld and made my first request for credit. I borrowed $50,000 initially and about $750,000 more over the course of the spring and summer. By Monday, August 18, we owed some $800,000 that the Bank knew about and we had written checks for an additional $500,000 which would be coming in for clearance that very week. Then, too, there were lots of people we had yet to pay.

The Bank hierarchy was more than a little agitated at this turn of events, and inquired of the elderly banker, with mid-winter arctic warmth, what, exactly, the Bank, a highly respected Wall Street institution, was doing financing some hippie drug fest in the Catskills. In addition, they asked, what, exactly, were the terms pursuant to which such large loans had been made? Here they received a nasty piece of news. The terms of the loan were fine. The Roberts family were fine people. Everyone and everything was fine. The only problem was that what with summer vacations, dilatory lawyers, and the disbanding of the Pony Express the agreement giving the Bank the all-important lien against the trusts had not arrived at the Bank yet, and thus was unsigned. The thing came down to our personal integrity and their good faith.

And that was how Woodstock was, more or less, financed.

John on Renee

The oldest employee of Woodstock Ventures—in all ways—was and still is a certain Renee (pronounced: *ree*-knee) Levine. Renee was and still is our bookkeeper and general factotum. She has the additional distinction of being the only person Woodstock has ever hired through an employment agency, because in March of 1969 no one on our staff had a friend who was a bookkeeper and because our accountant, Alex Jaffee, was hysterically fixated on the idea that we should have one.

In those carefree days, Michael, Artie, Joel, and I were in the habit of reporting every morning about ten to the apartment where Joel and I lived, there to sit around and plot our assault on the Youth of America. Around noon we would be joined by between three and eleven attractive young ladies who ostensibly were involved in putting together our hypothetical mail-order operation, which I shall discuss in merciless detail later on. Since in early March no one beyond our relatively small circle even knew that there was a festival being planned, the need for a mail-order crew eludes me. All I remember is that it existed—and was being paid—and that it and we were spread all over our living-room floor the day Renee Levine first walked in, having been dispatched to us by the XYZ Employment Agency for an interview.

My first impression of Renee was memorable. Tenaciously entrenched in her thirties, she was a woman of some five and one half feet, weighing between one and two hundred pounds. Her hair was red and curved out from her ears like a set of water buffalo horns, and she spoke a dialect of English indigenous to the uncharted area lying between the Gowanus Canal and Flatbush Avenue. She proclaimed herself a general ledger bookkeeper, which signifies, as best as I've been able to make out on the basis of our long association, that she has not been trained to perform any task that I assign her. "John," she will say, "you know I can't do that. I'm a general ledger bookkeeper, and you need a double-digit bookkeeper for that sort of thing."

Renee's voice is perhaps her greatest asset. It is an instrument of devastatingly seductive charm . . . over the phone. We get about fifteen calls a day from men who just want to hear her say "Good afternoon. Woodstock Ventures." (She rarely makes it in the morning.) In person, however, she has been known to set up a wail capable of creating fissures in the Tishman Building, and at the Festival she rendered a vital service to us, when all the telephones suddenly went dead, by standing outside our headquarters and yelling instructions to the site, three miles' distant.

Getting back to March of 1969, when Renee walked in she saw several young girls in various states of toplessness, two shaggy young men giggling over a funny cigarette, and then me and Joel. Since we looked vaguely human, she stopped in mid-bolt and asked if we were Woodstock Ventures. We said yes and then fired some questions at her that Alex Jaffee had given us to test her competence. Her answers were quick in coming and totally incomprehensible to us, so we hired her on the spot—or tried to. It seemed that Renee, while to all appearances in the robustest health imaginable, was suffering from a number of exotic and incapacitating diseases. She told us that her continued survival was due more to will power than to medical science, and asked very sweetly if she couldn't possibly start work in a month or so. "Or so" turned out to be another full month, and she didn't start doing whatever it is she still does for us until May 19.

Once Renee finally began work, it wasn't long before she became an indispensable part of our "organization." To the staff in general she was a mother figure. To Michael and Artie she was the Lachaiselike barricade that stood between them and reimbursements for their bizarre expense vouchers. To Joel and me she became a loyal and trusted friend, the keeper of the checkbook, the ear-splitting voice of sanity, and the shrewd Jewish *kvetch* who always knew a bum when she saw one—and she saw plenty. In her time, she stood up to lawyers, accountants, agents, rock stars, and even armed policemen. All of them, like us, got a lot more than they bargained for.

Joel on Curtain Call

Curtain Call, or Curtain Call Publications, Inc., as it was officially named, came up to see us from Philadelphia when we were a couple of months into our preparations. It was an organization with experience in the festival field, and it declared that it had assembled a package that would take most of the problems of throwing a bash for seventy-five thousand people off our shoulders. Bart Gluck, a weak-eyed roly-poly chap in his third or fourth decade, represented the combine, and he had a plan. He had several plans, in fact, depending on how much we wanted to budget. We gave him the we'll-think-it-over-and-get-back-to-you treatment, but after a few days, Bart, leaving nothing to chance, got back to us.

In those days we were humane to the point of simple-mindedness in business. We were suckers for any sharpie who intimated that he'd laid out a lot of time and effort on our behalf. Bart Gluck, for example, had made such a sincere presentation and kept calling us so persistently that we began to feel guilty about not giving him some of the work. We talked it over for a while, trying to figure out what we could safely delegate. One of the plans he had presented concerned media buying. It made no more sense than anything else he had proposed, but it touched on as innocuous an area as any then available. We chose his cheapest estimate and then cut it in half, figuring to start slowly and then build if he did a good job. We never built. Matter of fact, we began to cut back on Curtain Call's participation, and as its fifteen-percent commissions dwindled, Bart Gluck began to twitch.

He knew he was in no position to complain, and so he hit on a brilliant way to salvage himself some business. He had just been summoned from Philadelphia, again, to explain the most recent problems with the ad placements. He and I were seated on some uncomfortable chairs in one of our drab cubicles, and Bart went into action.

"Joel, I've got a great idea," he began modestly.

"Eh?" I responded.

"Look at these offices, man; they're gruesome. And it just so happens that we do outta-sight office interiors."

"How much?" I asked from a defensive crouch.

"Any size office, man. We did one in Philly that . . ."

"No, Bart. I mean: How Much?"

"Oh that. Yeah. Let me look around." And he rose to start measuring our bank account, returning to my office about an hour later.

"Dynamite!" he said.

"How much?"

"Well, you can go a lot of ways with this thing. Now take, for example . . ."

I stopped listening. It wasn't that I was against doing the offices. They were dirty, unpainted, poorly furnished, and generally seedy—a real embarrassment to us, in short. It was just that I was tired of listening to Bart's interminable spiels, and simply tuned out until I thought I heard him mention a figure.

"*How* much?"

"Well, the choice is up to you, of course, but for $15,000 we could do an excellent excellent job."

"I was thinking of $2,500."

We settled on $5,000, and the next day, or, in other words, before I could come to my senses, work was begun.

For the next several weeks, Bart's crew of long-hairs bustled about: measuring, painting, stuffing, and doing all the things one expects of interior decorators. Only Artie had the sense to specify what he wanted. The rest of us couldn't really be bothered with it, although it turned out later that we were definitely going to be.

Having ignored them after paying half the $5,000 as a deposit, we approached their completed work as we would have an unveiling. Bart came up specially from Philadelphia to show us around our new domain.

It was an eye opener.

The main office, which looked out onto 57th Street, had been transformed from a large sedate room in need of a rug and some paint into an ankle-defying maze of carpeted levels. Bart was especially proud of this room, with its risers and tiers, and we stumbled around in it for a while, trying every so often to relax against pillowish furniture-type objects which invariably threw us off balance. The carpet was a pale impractical blue except for one area, which had recently turned brown under the influence of a cup of coffee—the first of many. We agreed that it was a marvel of interior décor. Bart had managed to take an empty twenty-by-fifteen office and remodel it so that there wasn't even room for a small desk.

Fairly glowing with self-acclaim, Bart continued the tour down the corridor. Each of the smaller offices had been treated with a different color of some outlandish rainbow, and the two bathrooms were bright green and bright red, for hysterical and anal personalities respectively.

For me, the tour ended in Artie's office, or, more accurately, in the green bathroom, whither I sprinted immediately after looking at Artie's office. As I mentioned, Artie had conducted that particular mad scherzo himself, and it did not reflect well on the stability of his personality structure. As in front, levels had been used. The color scheme was yucky beige and zingy yellow, and the seating arrangement revolved around two bulbous violet lumps which had a tendency to cast their occupants to the floor. Beginning at the back wall, a room-sized diaphanous funnel of speckled gauze coiled around and above the chair-things and snaked toward a focus behind an enormous rosewood desk at the opposite end. There sat the room's creator and sole tenant: A. Kornfeld, Rock Impresario. The over-all effect was to make Artie appear about six inches tall, but the strong urge to inform him of this was overcome by a still stronger urge to visit the green bathroom.

Somehow the guys from Curtain Call sort of drifted apart from Woodstock Ventures for a while after the remodeling. But our thoughts turned to them every business day.

Working for Woodstock

Fourth Floor, 47 West 57th Street, Manhattan
Tuesday, April 29, 1969, 11:00 A.M.

A middle-aged man with pronounced Semitic features and, judging by his expression, an even more pronounced Semitic premonition of disaster, cautiously opens the door leading into a suite of offices. He pokes his head inside and surveys what is visible of the interior. Smoke fills the air, and an elusive odor of incense. In the dim light, the man can make out the form of a girl lying inert on the floor about ten feet away. He steps back into the stair well and pulls out a pocket diary to check his location. Then he notices the sign, WOODSTOCK VENTURES, INC., on the door. He sighs resignedly, straightens his tie, and gives the door a decisive push.

"Anybody here?"

The girl on the floor rolls languidly over onto her back and opens her eyes. "Hey, man," she says in caressing tones, "are you a narc?"

"My name is Jaffee," the man replies. "I'm a certified public accountant and I'm here to see Mr. Roberts."

The girl tilts her head like a month-old spaniel spying its first cat. "Mr. Roberts?" she says. "Didn't you know, man? He was killed in the war. Remember? Like, when Jack Lemmon threw Jimmy Cagney's palm tree into the ocean." She doubles up, giggling.

Jaffee takes out a handkerchief and wipes his forehead. At this moment, Michael Lang opens the door leading into the room just on his right. Inside, about dozen people can be seen sitting or lying comatose among a litter of cardboard boxes and envelopes.

Lang is on his way out. "What's shakin', baby?" he inquires of Jaffee as he floats amiably by. Jaffee only stares, recoiling as from an adder. Lang stops opposite him in the doorway, a slightly puzzled smile on his face.

"Roberts," Jaffee whispers hoarsely, as if he were flashing a crucifix at a vampire.

Lang takes in the situation and smiles the more. "If you're looking for John, he's down at the end of the hall in that last office."

Jaffee grimaces and nods, then maneuvers in a counterclockwise arc so as to give Lang as wide a berth as possible. The smiling eyes follow his progress until he achieves his desired heading and turns away. When he looks back, Lang has disappeared.

Moving down the corridor, Jaffee glances into the cubicles that open onto it. The people in the rooms seem to move in slow motion when they move at all, hypnotically intent on whatever tasks they are performing. "Either this is all an optical illusion," Jaffee thinks, "or I've stumbled into an aquarium stocked with humans."

The room at the end of the corridor is just as disturbing in its way as everything else he has seen thus far. It is a sort of seraglio after the manner of Dali. Mauve carpeting terminates in canary-yellow walls which terminate in their turn in folds of grayish gossamer hanging from a purely conjectural ceiling. Here and there are doughy-shaped lavender bulges reminiscent of conventional furniture. At the far end of the room, as in place as a space capsule in a Palladian drawing room, there is a low-slung rosewood desk. Behind this desk, his eyes roughly level with its top, John Roberts is sitting on the floor wearing a charcoal-gray business suit and a club tie.

"John!" Jaffee exhales in relief.

Roberts looks up, lighted Marlboro in place. "Hello, Alex," he says with a smile. "Come in. Pull up a bump."

Jaffee edges into the office's interior. "John, for God's sake! What are you up to around here? Who are all those people? Who's that girl on the floor? Who was that crazy-looking guy I saw on my way in? Why isn't there any light?"

John laughs. "I should have warned you, Alex. Woodstock Ventures has become a very hip organization."

"Hip shmip," says Jaffee. "What is going on here?"

"Well, it's really all very harmless. Those people up in the front are our mail-order staff. The other offices are for bookkeeping, publicity, money-counting, and like that."

"Everyone seems to be asleep or something."

"Now, Alex. Appearances are deceiving."

"There must be about fifty bodies out there!"

"Oh, that. Just the new generation. Fifty today, fifteen tomorrow, thirty the day after. A lot of those people don't even work for us. They're just hanging out. You know."

"No." Jaffee shakes his head. "I don't."

John smiles indulgently. "You worry too much, Alex."

"Yeah," says Jaffee. "Me and your father both."

John stops smiling. "Uh, look, Alex, about my father . . ."

"I know. I know. He already told me himself he didn't want to hear anything more about what you guys are doing. It upsets him. Besides, now you're my client, everything's confidential."

John resumes smiling. "Great. But there is one thing you can tell Dad. You can tell him that business looks good."

"Yeah yeah," says Jaffee. "Just gimme the books, and let's hope I can keep you afloat."

John laughs. "Honestly, Alex. Just you wait till the Festival. You'll see there was a method to our madness."

"Your madness I'm used to," says Jaffee, glancing toward the other offices. "It's other people's methods that worry me."

Joel on Gizzy

Not too long after we set up the Woodstock offices on 57th Street, we went into an intensive hiring phase. The cubicles that lined the corridor of our suite filled with gaily bedecked maidens and dudes of the hippie persuasion, many of them as inept as they were handsome. There were exquisite secretaries who were afraid of electric typewriters, mail sorters who were prone to disabling paper cuts, and file clerks who had never quite mastered the alphabet. Somehow this staff got the work done, while contributing greatly to the ambiance of the office.

For the most part, Jock and I, used to dealing only with legal and financial secretaries who were only an inch shy of having two feet in the grave, took the staff in stride. We did a predictable amount of ogling in the early weeks, but it never got out of hand, and about ten days after we had completed our hiring, a definitive conversation on the subject took place. We had finished up at the office and were on our way down in the elevator when Jock uncharacteristically suggested that we have a drink at Lun Far.

"Joel, my boy," he began as we sat down, "I think we should have a little talk about the philosophy of working in an office filled with pieces of ass. Now don't get me wrong. I don't claim to be an expert on this. But it seems to me that there's a time and a place for everything in life; a time for work and a time for play." Here he favored me with a pregnant pause and a penetrating gaze. "I think we can both agree that the office hours are a time for work, right?"

"Right."

"Right! Now I could be wrong about this, but I'm pretty sure that one's work life and one's play life should not overlap in any way, especially in our situation."

"What, may I ask, are you driving at?"

"Well, here it is in a nutshell: I think it would be a bad

idea for us to date any of our staff. Now please don't misunderstand. I'm not suggesting that you were thinking of it or anything. I just thought I ought to bring it up in order to avert a potential problem. You see?"

I felt that silence was in order.

"Look, Joel; it can get sticky. You start going out with one of the secretaries, see? And things are going fine, right? But then maybe she screws up at her job. And then you can't fire her because she's your girl friend. Or, what's worse, the two of you break up and there she is at the office every day, you know?"

"Yeah, I know. But what I don't know is why *I'm* being subjected to this lecture."

Jock caught something in my tone. "What are you suggesting, Rosenman?"

"Oh, nothing. I was just wondering whether you'd developed a secret fancy for one of our employees yourself."

My partner was offended. "You swine," he muttered. "You haven't even listened to a word I've been saying."

"*Au contraire,* dumpling; I've been hanging on your every sentence, waiting patiently for a fresh idea, an original thought, something that I hadn't already . . ."

"We're in agreement then?"

"Of course," I said, halfway out the door. "And thanks a lot for the drinks."

The following Monday, Artie Kornfeld moved his establishment into our suite. Never one to travel light, he brought with him two of his retainers from Capitol. Both were secretaries, but the similarities ended there. The typist and dictation-taker of the two was short, plump, and exceedingly mild. The phone-answerer number-dialer was something else entirely. She was Gizzy.

Gisela Bitros wasn't beautiful by contemporary standards, but then, contemporary standards weren't meaningful next to her. Her smile, which was continuous, brought peace to those on whom it shone. Her emanations were unambiguously warm and caring. Her outlook on life blended the essence of Henry David Thoreau and Swami Satchadananda. Also, she had nice boobs. When Jock met her, she smiled at him, and there was the sound of a large quantity of bricks falling.

Events moved rapidly. Throwing shyness and discretion to the winds, Jock lit after Gizzy like a comet. Soon they were an item. They took long leafy lunches in Central Park, where Jock was initiated into the then mysterious health-food culture. They began to see each other in the evenings. Gizzy lived in a small apartment on the upper East Side near our place, and it was a rare evening when Woodstock's president didn't deck himself out in some pungent velour shirt that Gizzy had urged him to buy and trundle over to 82nd Street, where She dwelt. Some nights he would come back late and some nights he wouldn't come back at all. On one occasion I was still up when he lurched into the apartment, his eyes glazed with Colombian, his ears ringing with acid rock.

"How was your evening?" I asked.

"Beautiful, man. Outta sight. Do you like these beads Gizzy got for me?"

"They're sure nice."

"They're beautiful," he corrected. "Beautiful." Then he caught himself. "Of course, they're just objects though, aren't they?"

"Huh?"

"You know; just material things. They're not really important."

"What is important, Jock?"

"Music is important. Have you heard Blood Sweat and Tears? Beautiful! Love is also important. *Everything* is important. Even you're important." And he danced off toward his room humming "I Am the Egg Man."

At the office, Gizzy occasionally made a mistake or three. She was adorably apologetic when corrected, but she was never corrected when Jock could intercede. Time and again my thoughts traveled back to the Treaty of Lun Far. Even at the age of twenty-six, however, I knew that one couldn't urge a friend to fall out of love.

The *deus ex machina* in this romantic melodrama was a

young man tall and meaty enough to be an important link in the defensive secondary of the New York Jets. His name was Ray. He had a sweet tooth for Gizzy and she for him, which all came as something of a surprise to Jock, who had never even seen the guy except in the sports pages. It wasn't that Gizzy didn't think he was worth mentioning. Rather, she was waiting until Jock was "beautiful" enough to rise above bourgeois possessiveness.

I guess she didn't wait long enough. How she could love him and another fellow, and maybe others besides, was something my traditionalist partner couldn't comprehend. He sought to shatter the paradox by demanding her undivided loyalty.

"You know that Gizzy's going out with some other guy?" he asked me one morning.

"You want I should lean on him, boss?"

"He plays defense for the Jets."

"Would you settle for an anonymous phone call?"

"This is no time for jokes, Rosenman. I've told her it's either him or me."

"I'm sure she'll make the right choice."

As it turned out, she ended up in Syracuse, New York with a third guy, whom neither Jock nor Ray had ever heard of. Odd; I always thought she had a sneaker for me.

John on Keith O'Connor and Tickets

The grand design of Woodstock called for me to supervise all ticket-selling operations as well as handle the general administrative duties I incurred as president of the corporation. I was well qualified for this chore, because I had once spent a full morning hawking raffle tickets for one of my girl friend's favorite charities.

Those unfamiliar with the subject may scoff at the problems involved in selling tickets to an event like Woodstock. Idiots! I had to spend the better part of a weekend's lunch hours in Las Vegas figuring out the innumerable complications.

Having established that the dates of the Festival were August 15, 16, and 17, we next had to price and package the tickets. This involved setting a price for a Friday, a Saturday, and a Sunday ticket, then a price for a Friday and Saturday ticket and a Saturday and Sunday ticket, and, finally, a price for a Friday, Saturday, and Sunday ticket. Anyone who wanted a Friday and Sunday ticket was out of luck, what with Fridays, Saturdays, and Sundays falling consecutively in Orange County.

Having established and priced our ticket packages ($7 for one day, $13 for two, and $18 for three), we then had to print up our tickets in various colors corresponding to price and grouping and also develop a code to make them difficult to counterfeit. The code turned out to be a bunch of stars and crescents and rainbows in various configurations, which had to be memorized, so that if a fellow presented a Saturday-Sunday ticket with the correct color and legend but the wrong grouping of stars and such, we would know his ticket wasn't genuine . . . and stomp the snot out of him.

Speaking of legends, we had to print a lot of information on the tickets, the purpose of which, other than to inform the purchaser of time and place, etc., was to remove all possibility of liability in the event of anything at all happening to the purchaser at or on the way to the Festival. We disclaimed responsibility for everything from acute flatulence to flat tires, including, by the by, the nonoccurrence of our event. In addition, the purchaser was informed in the smallest possible print that he was not allowed to do anything once he got to the Festival except sit absolutely still and breathe through his nose. More specifically, he was enjoined from taking pictures or making recordings of any kind, and also from violating any law that had ever been enacted in any jurisdiction since the time of Hammurabi. The penalty for noncompliance was immediate expulsion from the Festival site and/or imprisonment, and those of our patrons with access to electron microscopes would have been able to make out vague intimations of additional financial liability on their part if things in general did not go as well as expected.

With printing and coding completed, we next had to set up a system for distributing our tickets. We contacted some forty-five Northeastern head shops and boutiques in this connection and asked them if they would be interested in acting as sales outlets for Woodstock. We agreed to advertise their businesses as places where tickets to the Festival could be bought, and they agreed to sell the tickets and keep meticulous records. Every week they were to hand over their receipts and get a new batch of tickets to sell. Their compensation for doing this was to be five per cent of their sales. Simple. So simple that our crack team of legal experts was able to reduce the arrangement to several pages, incomprehensible to me, which invariably proved useless whenever our outlets failed to keep accurate records, burned to the ground, or floated off into the eighth dimension on a cloud of marijuana.

We also had the in-house mail-order operation for our ticket sales. All our commercials and advertisements mentioned an address for the customer to write to direct. When a request came in, accompanied by a check, we would deposit the check, wait for it to clear, and then send out the tickets. After August 1, we sent out the tickets immediately, time being crucial. Cunningly realizing our predicament, some low-lived late-purchasing miscreants had the nerve to stop payment on their checks.

We have your names, varlets.

Sometimes letters arrived with requests for information. These were dutifully read and answered. Other letters arrived bearing rude messages and suggestions, even threats. These were also read and, out of the good feeling born of the Aquarian Age, answered . . . in kind.

That was the ticket operation. I sat at its head, making policy decisions, tutoring the girls in the complexities of addition and penmanship, arguing with lawyers and outlet owners, and making good-sized deposits. My special assistant was a young man by the name of Keith O'Connor, a "ticket cat" Michael had recruited from the box office at the Fillmore East for my benefit. Keith was very helpful. He knew which of our potential outlets were sufficiently hip to appeal to our prospective clientele. He directly supervised our in-house mail-order staff. And he kept the precisely accurate daily sales records that our accountants and the IRS demanded.

I have many fond memories of Keith, a man whose major problem where I was concerned was that he bore the same name as my brother. It's a silly thing, I guess, but the name Keith, on humans, never fails to set my teeth on edge.

The thing I remember most about him was his tendency to fall into a depression every afternoon around three. For two hours he would sit Buddhalike on the floor and monotonously extol the virtues of goat farming in Italy. By five he would have convinced himself and at least two of his listeners of the force of his argument, and they would all resign en masse and troop down to the Alitalia office. There, the need for money would be impressed on them, and they would promptly troop back to Woodstock and demand raises. By then, however, it was past quitting time, and the project was abandoned until the following afternoon, and so on and so on ad infinitum.

Aside from all that, Keith was an honest and hard-working young guy. It's no exaggeration to say that he was responsible for selling tens of thousands of tickets and collecting hundreds of thousands of dollars. In fact, he was invaluable to us. I wish him the best of everything, and I was glad to hear a while ago that he had finally made it to Italy.

PROGRESS (?) REPORT: MAY 15

LAND: The Mills property, Wallkill

STAFF: Renee, ten ticket-sales people, several "consultants," between four and eleven secretaries, one publicity man

TICKET RECEIPTS: None

TALENT BOOKINGS: About ten acts. On the track of the Beatles, the Rolling Stones, Bob Dylan, and Donovan

ATTORNEYS: One in New York City; one in Wallkill

PORTABLE TOILETS: 1,000 on order from Port-o-San and Johnny-on-the-Spot

MONEY SPENT: $121,988

T HE SEEDS OF
S USPICION

Joel on Publicity

During the middle period of Festival preparations, when I was still capable of keeping my food down, I used to celebrate each new day with a cup of coffee and a toasted cheese Danish. Jock would sit across from me at his desk, washing down doughnuts with a bottle of Milk of Magnesia. Sometimes we would chat, but more often there would be a package from Burrelle's, our news-clipping service, to wade through.

We paid Burrelle's a medium-sized fortune to comb the nation's newspapers and magazines for any mention of the Woodstock Festival. Apart from occasional lapses which resulted in our receiving articles relating the saga of a flower festival in Woodstock, Ontario, or a piece concerning lumber supplies, the service was remarkably efficient.

Most of the nation's papers got their Woodstock news from either AP or UPI, so a great many of the clippings were simply duplicates of one another. One morning in June when I was about halfway through my Danish and most of the way through my first helping of Burrelle's, I came across one of these which I had to read twice.

"This is odd," I said to the gulping and chewing Jock.

"*You're* odd," he replied, and laughed uproariously, revealing a hideous mouthful of whitish carbohydrates.

"No, seriously, Jock," I said, giving him the benefit of the doubt, "there's something funny going on here."

"What are you talking about?"

I handed him the article I'd been reading and waited.

"Well?" I said at length.

"Well what?" he replied, as nimble as ever.

"Well, do you think it's the same festival?"

"Of course it's the same festival, you idiot. What the hell's the matter with you?"

"Read these," I said, tossing him my latest finds. "They're just like that one."

"I still don't get it, Joel," he said after glancing over them. "What do you mean, is it the same festival?"

"What I mean is, is this article from the *Arkansas Democrat* that talks about a festival being produced by Mike Lang and Artie Kornfeld an article about *our* festival, or some other Woodstock Music and Art Fair? Here's another one, from the Dallas *Times-Herald:* 'Co-promoters Mike Lang and Artie Kornfeld announced today . . .' When did *we* drop out?"

"Now, take it easy, Joel," Jock soothed. "Maybe it's just a mistake or something."

"Mistake, my ass. First it was the separate downtown office for Michael. Then we had to have three, count 'em, three publicity firms on retainer. Now all of a sudden it's Mike Lang and Artie Kornfeld, 'co-producers of the Woodstock Music and Art Fair'! Does that sound like a mistake?"

I tossed another package of Burrelle's gleanings over to him and opened one for myself. "Let's go through the rest of this stuff and see if we find any more 'mistakes.' "

We found plenty. After half an hour, we each had a stack of clippings that featured the Festival but omitted the names of two promoters. Jock had been slow to anger, although not for reasons of temperament. Now he was fuming.

"This is ridiculous," he ranted. "Did they think that we weren't going to notice?"

"I can't figure it out, Jock. I mean, I can't even see what they have to gain by it that's worth the risk. I think we should call Miles. Maybe we're missing something."

We were, but not in the way I meant. Apparently everybody in show business except Jock and me knew that credits and money were interchangeable. "It's obvious," Miles told us, "that the guys who become known as the producers of the legendary Woodstock Festival will be worth their weight in doubloons on August 18, if they're still alive. Show-business people kick and scream much more about the size of their names on the marquees than they do about the size of their salaries." He cautioned us to make sure that the whole thing wasn't a typographical error or something, or an oversight on the part of our publicity people.

"Typographical error. Humph!" I muttered while dialing the number of Wartoke, our press agents. Jock listened in on the extension phone.

"Janie, baby!" I said. (They always brought out the Max Bialystok in me.) "It's Joel of Woodstock."

"How ya' doin', Joel of Woodstock?"

"Jes' fine, sweet cakes. Say listen, honey, I notice that a bunch of press releases have gone out lately describing Michael and Artie as, like, the two and only producers of the Festival. You know anything about that?"

"I know everything about it. Artie called about two weeks ago with instructions on that. He said the four of you had agreed on it. Not so?"

"Just confirming. Just confirming," I said as casually as possible. "Thanks a lot. I'll talk to you later."

Jock was dialing before I put my phone down.

"What are you doing?"

"Calling Lang, fa Chrissake!"

"Don't."

"Why the hell not?"

"A number of reasons. First, we haven't really thought about what we want to say. Second, it's only ten-fifteen, so he's probably not at his office. Third, we're having a meeting with those two fuckers this afternoon, and I want to spring it on them in person."

Jock didn't need any more convincing. We spent the rest of the morning getting our case together and trying to psyche out what their reactions would be. By the time two o'clock rolled around, we were almost enjoying our outrage.

As George Armstrong Custer would have said, it didn't go exactly as planned. Michael and Artie breezed in around two-thirty, full of "Hey, man!"'s which Jock and I responded to with sneers from behind our clippings. I leaped first, and then Jock, but we never even got up a decent head of steam. They were too fast for us. They were so goddamn quick. In a twinkling, they convinced us that they had only told Wartoke to play down Jock's and my Establishment backgrounds in the releases. Wartoke had just gone too far, and, yes, it certainly *was* a bummer that ought to be cleared up right away, because we were the four Mothah-Muskefuckingteers, weren't we, marching toward August 15 and beyond, arm in arm. . . .

And then they left.

Jock turned toward me, eyes popping with frustration. "You just made a fool out of us, Rosenman."

"It's 'fools,' Jock, but otherwise I believe you're right . . . for the first time today."

"First time! Who do you think noticed this whole clipping thing in the first place?"

"What clipping thing?"

John on Food for Love—I

One June evening as Joel and I were, uh, relaxing over at Artie's apartment, we got to talking about the many-faceted problem of human excrement: its collection, storage, and disposal. The conversation, while practical in its intent, slowly turned philosophical, until we found ourselves holding forth on the great human cycles. Our discussion set me to thinking. Somewhere in the back of my mind there was something about excrement that was bothering me. Excrement . . . body wastes . . . wastes can't be used . . . what can be used? . . . non-wastes . . . Energy, Nutrients—FOOD!

"Oh, fellows," I shouted. "It has just occurred to me that we are going to have to arrange to feed seventy-five thousand people for three days."

"Far out!" said Michael, and everybody tittered.

"It's no laughing matter," I went on. "There aren't enough restaurants in all of Orange County to accommodate so many people. Besides, we're advertising camping, which means they'll be staying at the site: our guests—all of them—for three days! This is something we should get to work on right away."

The four of us went right into what passed for action in our milieu. We spent the better part of a week studying the problem. We talked to the people who cater Met and Yankee games. We spoke to the concessionaires at Madison Square Garden. We checked with nutritionists, hygienists, and food- and beverage-control agencies. We canvassed our lawyers and our lawyers' lawyers in order to get a fix on the legal complications food service would involve. At the end of almost five days of feverish and concentrated study, we had a plan: farm the whole thing out to someone else.

Pursuant to our decision to offer our customers a New World or Aquarian Shopping Esplanade, we had been selling space to concessionaires such as bead and trinket makers, leather dealers, etc., for $100 and ten percent of their eventual profits. Michael had hired a friend of his from Florida to cover this operation from our end. This friend, a certain Peter Goodrich, had numerous contacts in the food business and assured Michael that he could get us a concessionaire without any difficulty. Thus, by the time that we collectively decided that the food venture should be farmed out, Michael was able to state with his usual assurance, "It's already gone down." A month or so earlier, Joel and I might have accepted this and turned our attention elsewhere. But now it was June and a lot of things that, according to Michael, had gone down had been popping back up of late. So we decided to look into the whole food question on our own. Over the course of the next two weeks we talked to Restaurant Associates, Chock Full o' Nuts, and Nathan's Famous, among others. In each case they were interested, but in each case they were put off by the uncertainty of our status in Wallkill.* They told us that to provide food for the

*See pages 65–85.

numbers we were talking about would involve considerable time and expense, and they didn't want to go through all the preparations only to discover that the Festival had been called on account of hysteria.

Finally, Michael called me with a breakthrough. "Hey, man," he said, "Goodrich has found us some food cats."

"Great!" I said. "Who are they?"

"I don't know, man. But they're heavy. Peter has been speaking to them off and on for a couple of weeks, keeping them in reserve in case everything else fell through. They've been studying the problem and they've done some work on lining up suppliers and stuff. Thing is, we gotta close the deal with them, like tomorrow. They need bread and they've gotta get started. We'll meet 'em at Marshall's at eleven tomorrow. Gotta split now."

"Good-by," I said into a dead phone.

I tried to digest the news, examining it for pros and cons, and finally decided that it was mostly bad. One does not keep heavy cats in reserve. One does not have to finance heavy cats.

With a sense of mingled foreboding and desperation I presented myself for fleecing promptly at eleven the next morning. I was ushered into Marshall & Morris's minute waiting room, where I was soon joined by four people, three of whom looked like refugees from the Dugway Proving Grounds. The fourth was dapperly attired but had a lean and hungry face. He kept turning suddenly to his left and then his right, as if protecting his flanks from phantom molesters. I pegged him at once as a lawyer, and then my stomach did a greasy flip-flop as I realized that the three trolls with him had to be the food cats. They proceeded to confirm the fact by introducing themselves as 1) Charles Baxter, a tall comma-shaped man of about twenty-eight; 2) Lee Howard, shorter and squatter, with long Brillolike hair; and 3) Jeff Joerger, medium height, long hair, funky clothes, and a bizarrely designed filling in one of his upper front teeth. The fourth man, as I'd surmised, was their lawyer, Stephen Weingrad.

Paul Marshall, one of our myriad attorneys, had a large

comfortable office with a lot of paneling and deep couches and easy chairs scattered around. When he ushered us in, we ranged ourselves in a grouping of these chairs and got down to business. Weingrad made the presentation. It seemed that some weeks ago Peter Goodrich had approached Jeff Joerger with the idea for handling the food at the Festival. Joerger had lined up suppliers and taken on his two partners. The situation now was that the resulting cartel, though long on expertise, was short on start-up capital. In fact, they had no money at all.

I was disappointed but not surprised. Long months of work on Woodstock had accustomed me to dealing with the indigent. Still, unreasonably, I had hoped for more.

Weingrad was saying that they needed roughly $75,000 to pay for advances on the food they were going to sell. This money would also go toward wages, shipping, soft goods, and other food-purveying necessities. He proposed that Joerger *et al.* repay us the $75,000 and then split whatever came in thereafter fifty-fifty. It was such a preposterous scheme that I knew at once we were going to O.K. it. There was in Weingrad's manner that certain insouciance that spelled "Take it or leave it—but I know you'll take it 'cause you ain't got no choice." For the umpty-umpth time it was the Woodstock Ventures over-the-barrel malaise. I would have gotten down on my knees in tearful gratitude if just once we had been over the barrel without our business associates knowing about it. Not being over a barrel was out of the question. Having our associates over a barrel was, well, the stuff of dreams.

Weingrad's pitch was interrupted by the arrival of Michael's man Goodrich. Joerger, Baxter, and Howard greeted him enthusiastically. "Hey, man!" "Hey, man!" "Hey, man!" they said, bringing to mind fond memories of the Andrews Sisters. I, too, had been looking forward to Peter's arrival, since I wanted to know, among other things, what our alternatives were, but the joyous heying that resulted from his appearance told me that he was unlikely to be a source of disinterested information.

"Do we have any other possibilities open to us?" I whispered to him, just to make rout official.

"None, man. These are the only cats. Everyone else has passed."

And so it was that Woodstock Ventures agreed to advance $75,000 to its food concessionaires, build their booths, provide their plumbing and electricity, and guarantee them a minimum number of customers. Our *quid pro quo* from them remained to be seen. As a last-minute precaution, however, I managed to include a stipulation in our agreement that all checks had to be cosigned by us, and thus guarded against the possibility that our food cats might skip off with our funds to some hideaway for the unwholesome.

The deal was drawn up and signed by the end of the day, and I made another of my all-too-frequent calls to the Banker to let him know that a biggie would be coming through. That evening I received a call from Joerger informing me that, in keeping with the good vibes that had been established during the negotiations, he and his cohorts had decided to dub their little enterprise "Food for Love, Inc."

"Food for Money" would have been more appropriate.

Corporate Intrigue

The Woodstock Offices
Wednesday, June 4, 1969, 2:10 P.M.

Joel and Artie are talking to John in the front room of the Woodstock suite. Their intent, angry expressions afford a sharp contrast to the grotesquerie of the décor and the mask of apoplectic astonishment on John's face.

"Now wait just a second, Artie," John erupts. "Michael was very clear to Joel and me that he needed that downtown office because . . . well . . . because you and he didn't see eye to eye on a lot of things and he couldn't get any work done what with all the static."

"Dig it, man. Like, I appreciate your toning down what Michael said. But Joel and I leveled with each other yesterday about the whole business, and what Michael told you was that I was forever screwing things up and that he just couldn't get anything done with me looking over his shoulder all the time and getting in his hair. Right?"

John glances at Joel, who nods. "Well," he says, "I guess those were the words that Michael used. Something like that anyway. But what I don't understand is your telling me that he told you the same thing about us."

"It's too much, isn't it? Michael came on to me like, 'Gee, Artie, I gotta get a separate office. If any of my cats got a look at Joel and John, they'd freak right out.' And I'd say, 'Shit, Michael, your cats have seen straight people before.' And he'd say, 'It's not that they're straight, man. It's that they're so fucking unhip—about everything. They just can't get anything together.' And he went on like that."

"Well goddammit!" says John. "What kind of bullshit does he think he's trying to pull?"

"It's a bummer, isn't it? That's why I got here early for today's meeting. I want to confront Michael with this and I wanted you two to be in on it when I did."

"Damn right we're in on it. That little fuck!"

"Now steady, Jock," says Joel. "I was pretty steamed up, too, when I figured out what was going on, but let's hear what Michael has to say before we jump on him."

"Why the hell should we?"

"I don't know, Jock; due process or something."

Roberts snorts.

"Look. All I'm saying is that this looks pretty serious for the partnership, and before we blow the whole project sky high we ought to listen to what everybody has to say. Even Michael."

"Hmmph!" says John, and snatches up the New York Post. Joel looks at Artie and shrugs.

Promptly at two-thirty, Mike Lang walks in.

"Hey, guys," he says, all cheerful good nature. "What's shakin'?"

He is met by three stony glares.

"Hey! What's with all these vibes?" He looks from face to face. "Feels like there's some really bad shit going down."

"We've just been comparing notes, Michael," says John. "It seems you don't think too much of us."

"Too much of who, man?"

"Any of us. Me, Joel, Artie."

"What are you talking about, man? What's this all about?"

"Oh, for Christ's sake, Michael!" Joel breaks in. "You know damn well what this is all about. You've been telling Artie that John and I are incompetent fuck-ups, and you've been telling us the exact same thing about him. Now suppose you explain to us just exactly what the hell is going on around here."

"There's nothing going on, Joel. I just want to get the gig done."

"What the fuck does that mean?" John spits.

"It means I just want to get the gig done. That's all. Isn't that what we all want?"

"Yeah," says Artie, "that's what we all want."

"Well then," asks Michael with an angelic smile, "what's the problem?"

"What's the problem!" John explodes. "How the hell are we going to get the gig done if you keep stirring up the shit all the time?"

"Wait, man," says Artie. "I don't think we're being entirely fair to Michael."

John's mouth drops. "Whaaaat?"

"No, seriously, man. I can dig what he's saying."

"Now hold on a minute, Artie," Joel says. "You were just as pissed off as we were about this whole thing a minute ago. What the fuck is going on?"

"It's just that I see what Michael's saying, man. We're all in this together, and if we run around worrying about who said what to who every second, well we're just gonna fuck ourselves."

"Right on!" seconds Michael. "Thing is, we've all been farting around too much; not working hard enough. And the result is that we've started getting hung up on nonessentials."

"Yeah!" says Artie.

"Speaking for myself," Michael continues, "I'm glad this

whole thing happened. I think it's cleared the air and showed us what's really important."

"Me, too," adds Artie. "I'm going out of here after this meeting and really get that publicity program moving."

"Great!" says Michael. "I'm going up to the site and make damn sure that stage is progressing. Joel?"

"Huh? Oh. Right. Well, I'm sure John and I will keep things rolling on our end."

"Terrific, man!" Michael applauds. "This meeting's been a real blessing in disguise. I'm headin' up for Wallkill right away —while the flavor lasts."

"Far out!" says Artie. "I'm gonna get on the phone to Bart Gluck and make sure he gets his ass in gear about those radio spots."

"Five, baby!" cheers Michael, and he and Artie give each other's palms a resounding slap.

"See you tomorrow, guys," says Artie as he heads out the door.

"Yeah. *Adios*," says Michael, a smiling half a step behind him.

The door slams and the office is suddenly quiet. John and Joel exchange long questioning stares, first at the door, then at each other.

"I feel like I just had my pocket picked," Joel says at last.

"Me, too," John replies. "And the worst of it is that I'm not even all that sure that I still want to get the gig done."

PROGRESS (?) REPORT: JUNE 15

LAND: The Mills property

STAFF: Renee, forty ticket-sales people, additional consultants for talent, security, logistics, one stage manager, fifty construction workers at the site

TICKET RECEIPTS: $169,338

TALENT BOOKINGS: Almost complete. Beatles, Stones, *et al.* abandoned as too expensive

ATTORNEYS: One in New York City for Woodstock Ventures; one in New York City for film and record contracts; one in Wallkill

PORTABLE TOILETS: An additional 500 ordered to aid Wallkill public relations

MONEY SPENT: $251,102

UNMAKING WALLKILL

John on the No-Smoking Memo

One of the many problems we faced in the area of employee relations was the all-consuming love of our staff for marijuana. Such a passion among normal people would not have caused us much anxiety, since pot's illegality could have been counted on to foster a degree of discretion in its use. Among those elements of society from which Woodstock recruited its labor force, however, grass smoking with a reckless disregard for the statutory amenities had, by 1969, become a sort of badge of honor. It had even gotten to be a kind of matadorial contest, in fact, and the more blatant your offense, the better your high. Things had reached a point where a number of the more firmly established heads simply could not get off more than ten yards from a police station, and the most coveted coup de grass of all was to roll, ignite, and consume a joint while you were being arraigned for picketing. Of course, the fact remained that getting caught wasn't cool, but it wasn't serious either, since all you lost were style points. And besides, getting busted gave you something to rap about the next time you got stoned.

Those of us in positions of responsibility, *i.e.*, with something to lose, had to tread lightly on the grass issue. On the one hand we were promoting a celebration of the Aquarian Age, and our patrons fancied themselves street people and flower children. On the other hand we were a New York corporation capitalized at $500,000 and accounted for by Brout Isaacs & Co., tenth-largest body of CPAs in New York City.

The dilemma was a cruel one, and we turned as one man to the keen legal intellect of Joel Rosenman for a solution.

"I think I have an idea," he said, after a few minutes of profound concentration. "What we'll do is, we'll circulate a strict No-Smoking memo supposedly directed at our staff, but really calculated to make an impression on the Wallkillese. It should read something like: 'It has recently come to our attention that some Woodstock employees are experimenting with the use of marijuana. We are shocked that such lawlessness should exist within our corporate family. Anyone found using marijuana or any other illicit substance will be immediately dismissed and their offense reported to the proper authorities.' Now once this memo is issued, we'll tell the staff that it's only a public-relations hype, but we'll ask 'em to be cool all the same so we don't screw things with the locals. Then we'll plaster the thing all over Wallkill and convince everybody what good citizens we are."

This bit of Rosenmanic inspiration was greeted by those of us in positions of responsibility with wild one-handed applause and the usual obligatory choruses of "Heavy," "Far out," "Oink," etc. The very next day the memorandum was drafted and typed, and within a week it had been posted. We sat back and confidently awaited the community's response.

It was not long in coming. First, one of our sweetest, most incompetent young secretaries picked up a ringing office phone and heard: "Who do you mother-effing hebe commie hippie bastards think you're fooling with this 'No-Smoking' shit? We know what you freaks are up to, and if you ain't outta this town real soon there's gonna be a lot of long hair and fillings lying around on the roads."

"Oh dear!" she said.

Then our local attorney called to tell us that the people of Wallkill had been under the impression that it was our prospective audience that had the drug fetish. Until our memo it had never occurred to them that the plague was among them already, and an emergency town meeting had been called to deal with the crisis.

Finally there was our staff's reaction. To their credit, they quit smoking on the job almost immediately and instead took to getting stoned before heading off to work in the morning. Many of them didn't turn up till the autumn.

Michael, Artie, and I had much to be pleased about, therefore, in connection with Joel's brainstorm, and we thought a good way to show our appreciation would be to report him to the proper authorities. We decided against it in the final analysis though, because by that time the proper authorities were out hunting for our heads.

John on Felix Lourie

One evening in June I was having a drink with a couple of friends and holding forth, as usual, about the problems involved in putting on our little rock pageant. In particular, I was discussing for the umpteenth time the elaborate toilet facilities we intended to provide for our patrons.

"But all this talk of bathrooms is beside the point," I said morosely, interrupting my standard disquisition on hippie turd.

My friends regarded me warily. Bathrooms beside the point? He must be going bad. The strain is telling. Shit must out. I knew their thoughts.

"Yes, beside the point. Given the fact that we may not even have a festival site by next week, toilets have taken a decidedly back seat in our thinking."

"But didn't you tell us just last month that they loved you up in Wallkill?"

"That was last month. This month they started hearing some of our advertising about the gathering of the tribes and the celebration of the Aquarian Age, and the pitchforks started coming down off the walls. You see, when we first approached the town, we hit 'em with an art fair and music idea; a little folk, some classical, maybe some sedate rock—and a jot of art. Now they've picked up some of the rumbles from the underground and they're getting a little hysterical. They want us out of there."

"What are you going to do about it?" I was asked.

"Well, I spent most of today with our PR people outlining plans of attack on the soft underbelly of Wallkill. Our head publicist's ace in the hole turned out to be some washed-up baseball player he wants to send up there for the rest of the summer to conduct a baseball clinic for the local kids, courtesy of Woodstock Ventures. The first problem with that plan is that the kids are already on our side. The second problem is that the idea stinks. It's ineffective and embarrassing. It's also transparent." I paused. "I think we'll probably do it."

My friends stared at me in disbelief. Finally one of them said, "You're right, it stinks. It won't work. You try that and you might as well close up shop tomorrow. You don't need baseball players. You need some kind of political pressure, an endorsement from the State Arts Commission or something. Maybe you could get Orange County to proclaim the Festival a local economic blessing. The important thing is to get a little political muscle. That's the way things work, you know. Get the pols on your side and the rubes won't touch you."

It was brilliant, I thought, and so simple. I raced to the phone to call Joel and tell him I had the solution to our problems, but then I remembered it was Monday, his needlepoint night.

Who to call and share my good news with? A light went on in my head. I recalled that our attorney, Miles Lourie, had once introduced me to his father, Felix, and told me that he was politically well connected if we should ever need that sort of thing. I called Miles and told him I had to get in touch with his father. He told me to come to his office the next morning around ten. "Dad will be waiting for you."

The following day Joel and I went over to Miles' and there, waiting for us as advertised, was Felix, a short, powerfully built man of about sixty-five. He had a ruddy pink face, a shock of white hair, and the most brilliantly twinkling little blue eyes. He also had a soft high-pitched voice and a very careful

way of enunciating every syllable of every word he said. The
effect of this mannerism was to make one tire of his conversation
very quickly.

Felix's favorite subject was the past. He had a host of
memories. That particular morning he greeted us with bone-
crushing handshakes and then used the occasion of our pained
yelps to tell us how he had gotten himself the nickname "The
Little Bull." By lunchtime he had taken us through the better
part of the nineteen-thirties, when I broke in to explain our
predicament. I went into some detail and, on concluding, sat
back and awaited a reaction. Felix seemed plunged in thought.
We waited. Finally the telltale purr of a snore broke the silence.
Felix was napping. We glanced at each other, rose to leave, and
accidentally woke him with our movements.

"Boys," he said, "I have an idea." With that he winked
and smiled.

"What is it, Felix?" I asked with some weariness. "No
parables. No riddles, please. Just tell us straight."

He managed to look offended. "Youth and its impatience,"
he said. "When I was young . . ."

"FELIX!!!"

"Oh, very well," he said. "Malcolm Wilson."

"Who's he?" said Joel.

"The Lieutenant Governor of New York," I said. "What
about him?"

"I know him," said Felix. "I can get us an appointment
with him."

"What'll that do?" I asked.

"John, he's a very important man in this state. He can
help us. I'm sure of it."

"Can he get the state to endorse our festival?" I asked.

"Well, I don't know about that," said Felix, "but I'm sure
he will be helpful to our cause."

Several hours later he called me to tell me that Wilson, as
a special favor to him, had agreed to see us at his New York
office the following day at eleven.

The next morning, Joel and I met Felix outside the Lieu-

tenant Governor's office on West 55th Street. He started right
in. "Now I know you boys want to set the world on fire this
morning, but that's not the way it's done. Patience and good
manners will win the day. Lieutenant Governor Wilson is a very
busy man, and he has consented to this visit as a very special
courtesy to a very old friend. Just go on in there, tell him your
problem, and listen. Anything else would be a terrible embarrassment to me."

I had the sinking feeling that we were embarked on a
colossal waste of time.

A male secretary ushered us into the great man's office,
and as he and Felix grabbed each other in greeting, I looked
around the room. The walls were hung with plaques and cita-
tions, mostly from religious groups. Malcolm was a good conservative and an even better Catholic. The walls told me that we
had come to the wrong place.

We were introduced, shook hands, and sat down. Wilson
said, "My good old friend Felix has told me that you fellows are
putting on some kind of music fair in Orange County this
August. I'm sure you understand that the state can't become
involved in private commercial enterprises. The Lord knows we
have little enough money to spend on the arts in this state. Why,
as recently as last week I was talking to Monsignor . . . " and
here he drifted off into a completely irrelevant little story that
my memory has mercifully failed to retain. I stole a look at
Felix. He was entranced, sitting erect in his chair and hanging
excitedly on Wilson's words. Occasionally he looked at me and
nodded as if to say, "See? I told you he could help."

The voice droned on. Finally I could stand it no longer.
"Mr. Wilson . . ." I began.

A gasp from Felix. "It's *Governor* Wilson, John. We say
Governor." And, turning to His Governorness, "I'm *awfully*
sorry."

"That's O.K., Felix. What is it, young man?"

"Look, uh, sir," I said, "we're not interested in money.
What we want is a letter from the state or yourself or someone of
importance endorsing our festival. That's all."

Silence.

Finally, in a voice that implied that he thought we had come there to hear his religious reminiscences, Wilson said, "You must understand that we can under no circumstances fund or [meaningful pause] endorse a private venture such as yours, or, in fact, any privately financed operations."

On that note the audience was concluded.

As soon as we were outside, Felix turned on me. "John, that was an inexcusably rude outburst."

"I know, I know," I said. "But we just weren't getting anywhere."

Felix was aghast. "How little you know. How little you know. The meeting was going so perfectly, and now . . . Now, well, all I can suggest is that I set up an appointment in Albany with one of Governor Rockefeller's executive secretaries, a man by the name of Peterson, and see what help he can offer. It's possible that may retrieve the situation."

"O.K., Felix," I said. "But make sure before we go up to Albany that he knows exactly what we want."

"Please, young man, leave it in my hands," said Felix, adding proudly, "Didn't I get you in to see the Lieutenant Governor?"

Thursday night he called to say that he had set up a meeting with Peterson for the very next morning. I was to meet him at La Guardia at 8:30 A.M.

I dutifully arrived at the airport at the appointed time, and together Felix and I boarded a creaking old Allegheny or Ozark Airlines DC-3 or something. As soon as we were settled in our seats, I got an unpleasant inkling of what the day held in store for me. "John," said Felix, "I really know very little about this Woodstock Festival. Miles rarely discusses his work with me now that I'm semiretired. Tell me a bit about it."

I gave him a quick run-through, but that didn't satisfy him. He had prepared a list of questions, which ranged from the inevitable toilet logistics to water, electricity, land gradations, and rain insurance. He never really listened to my answers, I'm sure, but he nodded alertly while my voice was going on and frowned thoughtfully whenever it stopped. Occasionally I would try to still the flow of questions by saying, "Look, Felix, I think about this stuff every day. I was kind of hoping that today for maybe a few hours I could relax and take my mind off it. You know."

"If you stop thinking about it, you may forget it altogether," he replied. And that was that. All the way from New York, through the arrivals building, in the cab, on the steps of the Capitol building, and on into Peterson's office, where, at last, he subsided.

Peterson turned out to be an attractive and bright young guy. I related my sad story, bluntly told him what we needed, and asked his opinion. He answered that he couldn't get us a direct and specific endorsement, but he thought he could get us a letter from the Governor's office praising artistic endeavors in general and welcoming us specifically to New York.

It wasn't much, I thought, but it was something. If we were clever, we might be able to use it to our advantage. The Wallkill Town Supervisor was a Republican, after all.

Peterson told me the letter would be on my desk as soon as possible, perhaps by Tuesday. I thanked him, grabbed Felix, and fled before The Little Bull could deliver himself of the excruciatingly sycophantic monologue I knew from his glassy expression he had been concocting throughout the meeting. I trundled him out the door, down in the elevator, and out into the sunlight, but there he dug in his heels.

"John, that was a terrible terrible thing we did."

"*What???*"

"We were rude, inexcusably rude. We should have invited that nice young man to lunch. In fact," he added, turning around, "it's not too late. I'm going back up there right now."

"No, Felix, puh-lee-yuz," I shouted. "I've got a lot to do back in the city. There's a plane in forty minutes. We can catch it. No no, Felix, please nooooo."

He was already back inside beetling toward the elevators. I wheeled, I pleaded, but he had it fixed in his mind that an injustice had been done, and he was going to rectify it. Small-arms fire couldn't have stopped him. I tried to comfort myself by reflecting that Peterson was probably a) too busy, b) previously engaged, c) not interested, or d) already eating.

It was e) none of the above, so we went to lunch.

It was a predictably dismal affair. Peterson sat amazed and listened to Felix recite his past glories. I drank.

With the coming of dessert, Felix decided to hurdle the present and launched into a spectacularly imaginative description of our impending festival, using as his sources our morning's conversation on the plane and a dimly recollected visit he had made to Tanglewood two years earlier. None of it made sense. At the high points in his narrative, he would grab his Scotch sour, jump to his feet, and trill "To High Adventure!" By then I was well past caring, but Peterson kept looking around nervously to see if anyone from his office was in the vicinity. Once the bill was paid and we were out on the street again, however, he walked over to me and whispered, "Don't worry. He's a sweet old man. It's going to work out fine." It was nice of him, but I was not reassured.

Felix and I hopped a cab to the airport, he gabbing incessantly about what a fine thing we had done and how it was always best to make the polite impression—I'd soon see, etc. At the airport we boarded the same sort of plane we had taken in the morning, but with one vital difference. Whereas all the seats on the way up had been side by side, in this aircraft there were some facing each other. I took one and Felix took the one facing me. I figured that the distance between our faces combined with the engine noise would make conversation impossible.

I was wrong.

He shrieked over the din in my direction. When I would pretend not to have heard whatever he had just finished saying, he would poke me and nod expectantly, waiting for my answer. It went on like that until I hit on the stratagem of pretending to be asleep. During a brief pause in his flow, I closed my eyes. Nothing. It was working. Thirty seconds passed. Suddenly I felt an insistent tapping on my left knee. I ignored it. The tap turned into a jab. It hurt. I opened my eyes. Felix, bowing to the racket of the engines, was using sign language to ask his question.

He carefully laid the bottom edge of his left hand on my knee so that it formed a little barrier. He then used the fingers of his right hand to simulate something running at it. When the fingers arrived at its base, they left the ground (my knee) and flew up and over. He repeated this little bit of business twice, then looked up at me, cocked his eyebrows, and waited for my comments.

I thought I was dreaming. I said nothing.

What would *you* have said?

Finally he did it all over again, and I gave up. "What is it, Felix?" I asked. "Do you have a question?"

"The gates," he hissed triumphantly. "How are you going to keep them from jumping over the gates?"

To drive home his point more forcefully, he ran through his demonstration yet again.

I very nearly broke down.

Felix looked at me for a moment and then laughed. He took his right index finger, pointed it at his temple, laughed again, and made a little twirling motion. Then he pointed the digit at me.

Felix wanted only $3,000 for his services. We settled with him for something less.

Peterson's letter did us no good in Wallkill, but it did arrive just in time to present to the Town Board of White Lake.

They were, by and large, Democrats.

Democracy in Action

The Town Hall, Wallkill, New York
Thursday, June 12, 1969, 7:45 P.M.

The room that roughly two months earlier had been nearly empty as the Zoning Board of Appeals gave Joel and John its blessing is now jammed, and a loud stertorous murmur runs through the assembled crowd. It is a heterogeneous collection of

people: a large hard-hat contingent and a group of their visibly
alienated adolescent children sporting longish hair and incipient
clusters of acne; the Woodstock contingent, heterogeneous in
and of itself, with Lang and Roberts representing the extremes;
local professional people, prominent citizens dutifully projecting
an air of troubled impartiality; a covey of conspicuously slick
out-of-town attorneys, here to protect the amalgam of hopelessly
tangled interests Woodstock now encompasses; and the Wallkill
Town Board, headed by Supervisor Jack Schlosser, which is
seated at a makeshift dais and fluctuating between complacency
over the sudden importance being attached to its deliberations
and nervousness over the size and vehemence of the crowd.
Nervousness seems to predominate, however, largely because
the board includes the three members of the Zoning Board of
Appeals who granted Woodstock permission to come to Wallkill
in the first place.

Joel, John, Michael, and Woodstock's counsel are huddled
together.

"The natives are restless," says John.

"Take it easy, man," Michael says serenely. "There's no
sweat. Like I keep telling you, it's already gone down."

John snarls and lights another cigarette.

"My stomach hurts," says Joel.

"I think it's marvelous," says the attorney.

Joel and John turn to stare at him. He is beaming expan-
sively over the assemblage. "Just marvelous," he repeats. "Look
at this. It's America. Democracy in action. The political process
at the grass roots. America!"

John's face turns a shade of indigo. Joel takes a long
look at the lawyer and then sadly shakes his head. Lang smiles
seraphically. "Right on, man!" he says. "America."

Town Supervisor Schlosser bangs his gavel. His six colleagues on the board turn to face the audience, which, to the
accompaniment of a few squeaks of chairs and hushings of
children, gradually subsides into silence.

"Well, we seem to have some problems with this, uh,
Woodstock matter before us."

"We damned well do!" comes a voice from the back of the room, seconded immediately by an angry approving buzz.

"Now, folks . . ." says Schlosser as the board members shift uneasily in their chairs. He decides to let the admonition go at that. "I understand that George is representing the Woodstock people. Do you want to kick things off, George, and tell us why exactly this, uh, A-quarian Art and Music Festival isn't going to be a real disaster for our town."

"Excuse me, Jack, er, Mr. Schlosser, but I don't think we should get the wrong impression. I mean, there's no question of any sort of disaster happening, and we're certainly prepared to give you some reports today on preparations for the Festival which should quiet any doubts on that score."

Schlosser nods. "Fair enough, George. I haven't seen those reports, of course, but I hope they take into account the feelings of people around here about this whole thing."

"Well, they're certainly intended to. Now, back on April 14 when the ZBA gave Woodstock the go-ahead to begin preparations, my clients promised . . ."

"Excuse me, George," Schlosser interjects, turning to the man on his immediate left. "Ed, wasn't it your understanding from what was said back in April that all that was planned was a little art exhibit or some such thing?"

Ed squirms. "Well, yes. I guess so. That was pretty much what they told us—more or less."

George breaks in. "Now hold on a minute, Ed. Excuse me, Jack, but I think a lot more was said than that."

Schlosser scratches his head. "Well, gee, there must be a record of the meeting. You did make a record, didn't you, Ed?"

"Yeah," Ed says defensively. "Of course we made a record. A couple of guys stood up and said they were going to have some people up here, and so on. We didn't go into it much more than that."

"Well why the hell not?" several people in the audience want to know.

Schlosser bangs his gavel. "Folks! Please! George, let's just leave aside that whole April ZBA meeting. I know I brought it up, but let's just forget it and concentrate on the present for now. Go ahead with what you were saying."

"Thank you, Jack. All I really want to point out is that Woodstock is made up of decent people with fine credit references who simply want to bring a music festival up here to Wallkill. And I don't think it reflects credit on us that we're prepared to throw them out—or some of us are anyway—just because we've heard a few rumors that make us nervous. Now a lot of petitions have been circulated by the Concerned Citizens Committee and a lot of angry words have been spoken, but I think you owe these people the courtesy of a hearing, and I think you should listen to what they have to say with an open mind, because they've done a lot of work preparing reports and surveys just so they could explain to you exactly what it is they're planning."

George sits down and the room rumbles mutinously.

"Thank you, George," says Schlosser. "I believe the first person to speak for Woodstock will be Mr. Michael Lang."

As Michael stands up there is an audible sucking in of breath, and a by now familiar voice from the back shouts, "Did you say Mr. . . . or Miss?"

The room erupts in laughter and Michael permits himself a secret smile. After order is restored, he proceeds to discuss the types of entertainment that the Festival will feature, emphasizing, perhaps unduly, painting and bead-selling. It is one of his usual uncannily articulate presentations, and by the time he finishes, the once heckling audience is grudgingly allowing him a measure of respect. "Are there any questions?" he asks.

"Yeah," says a beefy middle-aged man wearing a Cortland State Teachers College sweatshirt. "You've done a lot of talking about the people who are going to be playing the music, but what we want to know is: what sort of people are gonna be coming up here to listen to it?"

"Music lovers, I would think," says Michael with a grin, and the audience chuckles.

"Well, Mr. Lang, we all of us here like music as well as

the next fellow, but the people we're talking about seem to like music—and marijuana and opium, too."

"Aw, cripes!" says one of the dissident preteens. "You people are all paranoid."

"You keep a civil tongue in your head, Alvin Brewster!" comes a shrill woman's voice from near the front.

"Well, sir," says Michael, ignoring the *tableau vivant*, "as you know, those drugs are illegal, and I don't think that the people who will be coming to our festival are criminal types in any way, shape, or form."

"They may not be criminal types," says the beefy man, "but they sure do like drugs, I betcha."

This sally is greeted with loud sustained applause and a few amens. The commotion subsides only after Schlosser has very nearly driven his gavel through the table.

Michael responds to several more argumentative questions and then sits down. He is followed by Joel, who discusses traffic flow; John, who discusses financing; and the New York attorney, who discusses various legal safeguards that are being taken. Then the nuts and bolts of the Festival are gone into. One Woodstock employee talks about parking arrangements. A second goes into the various community-relations measures being contemplated. Both are hectored by angry shouts and accusations which Schlosser manages to restrain only with difficulty. Maps and charts and graphs and mock-ups are brought out one after another to illustrate and support what is being said, but the hostility mounts. Wes Pomeroy, Chief of Security for the Festival and former Special Assistant to Attorney General Ramsey Clark, gives a sober, reasoned summary of the law-and-order arrangements. He, too, is subjected to constant badgering and to questions like "What about those three people that got killed down at the concert in Atlanta?" and "What are you going to do about all the nudity that'll be going on?"

The final speaker for Woodstock is a wiry bantam-sized man named Mel Lawrence, Chief of Heavy Construction. He rises to speak virtually concealed by the stacks of blueprints and flow charts that he, along with two assistants, is lugging to the front of the room. A blackboard is wheeled in as an additional visual aid, and Lawrence is ready to roll.

He begins by giving a detailed explanation of how the construction for the Festival is being managed. He then discusses in turn sanitation, water supply, electricity, noise levels, and sundry associated issues, galvanizing—or mesmerizing—his listeners in the process. They find his consummate practical savvy impressive, and when he finishes and it's time for their hitherto loaded questions, their voices betray a distinct note of diffidence.

"Say, Mr. Lawrence, how can you be so sure that your sewerage flow is going to bypass populated areas?"

"Well, look at this diagram, for God's sake. Don't you remember anything I told you. Sewage flow is *downhill*—always downhill. You got that? We had this setup in Hawaii, for example. Boy, you should have seen it! Straight as a die right down into the Pacific. It was beautiful. There's no problem at all about this."

"Uh, Mr. Lawrence, what are you going to do to protect livestock in the area?"

"Oh, Christ! What do you do for a living anyway? You're a farmer, right? Well how long have you had a farm, you shnook? I just finished telling you two minutes ago that the whole site is ringed with fresh pasturage. How many cows do you know that are gonna go skipping past a field full of grass in order to listen to rock music?"

The crowd laughs and applauds.

"Well," says Schlosser, "I guess everybody's had a chance to have his say. We've got our new local law pending here and I understand that the Concerned Citizens are trying to get a court order, so I guess we haven't really settled anything. As I said, though, we've all had a chance to express our views, and if there's nothing else to be discussed, the meeting's adjourned."

Chairs scrape across the floor, parents call to children, voices rise in side arguments here and there across the room. John and Joel huddle briefly with George.

"Well, George, how do you think we did?" John asks.

"Well," says George, "Mel sure made a good impression."

"That bad, huh?" says Joel.

George shakes his head and shrugs. "We did as well as could be expected," he concludes, "but whether that'll be good enough, I just don't know."

It is an unjustifiably optimistic assessment.

Dinner at the Four Seasons

99 West 52nd Street, Manhattan
Wednesday, July 2, 1969, 9:15 P.M.

Joel and John, with dates, and their Media Sound partners, with wives, are celebrating the long-awaited opening of the studio. They are engaged in cheerful badinage when a waiter approaches carrying a telephone.

"Mr. Rosenman?"

Joel raises his hand and the waiter places the phone on the table in front of him.

"Hello . . . Oh, hi . . . Yes. Thanks. What's the news?"

All the people at the table except John carry on with their merrymaking as Joel talks. John sits silent, glaring balefully at him.

"If that was anything to do with the Festival, I don't want to know about it," he says the moment the call is completed.

Knowing his man, Joel simply nods and begins talking with his date. This has its intended effect.

After several minutes during which John neither eats a bite nor speaks a word, the conversation round the table is brought abruptly to a halt.

"What the hell was that phone call about, damn it?"

John has spoken a touch more loudly than is perhaps customary among restaurant patrons, and upward of several dozen eyes turn suddenly in his direction. An embarrassed giggle fleets over his features, and then a frown. "Who *was* it?" he asks in a fierce whisper.

"That was our answering service," Joel replies.

"And . . . ?"

"It was about the Festival. You don't want to know about it."

John restrains himself with difficulty. "What about the Festival?"

Joel clearly doesn't have his heart in his teasing. Equally clearly, however, he doesn't relish the prospect of repeating what he has just heard.

"I asked Goldstein to call the service when the Zoning Board got through meeting." Stanley Goldstein was Michael's assistant.

"And you told the service to call you here? During *dinner!*"

Joel shrugs. "Sorry. I was curious."

"Christ! We're supposed to be celebrating."

"Yeah."

For a while no one speaks. The six noncombatants at the table take shelter in their food, occasionally sneaking brief glances at Joel, who seems absorbed in melancholy, and at John, who seems primed to throw a fork.

Then the stillness is shattered. "Goddammit, Joel! What happened?"

Joel looks at John and sighs. "Well, Jocko, what happened was that the board passed the new ordinance and the Concerned Citizens are taking us to court."

"Oh SHIT!" says John, garnering for himself the undivided attention of eight surrounding tables.

A waiter suddenly appears. "Is anything wrong, sir?"

"Huh?" says John. "Er . . . yes. I'd like a glass of water."

The waiter deftly indicates a brimming tumbler approximately three centimeters to the right of John's tournedos Rossini. "You wish *another* glass, sir?"

"Uh? Oh! Well. I see. Heh heh. No, thank you. My error. Excuse me."

The waiter frigidly withdraws. Everyone at the table appears to be experiencing difficulties with their undergarments.

"Sorry, all of you," says John. Then he looks at Joel. "That just about wraps it up for Wallkill, doesn't it?"

"Yes," agrees Joel with a tired nod. "That pretty much wraps it up."

John looks at the sympathetic faces around the table and smiles a little smile. "Oh well," he says. "There's always Carnegie Hall."

Excerpts from Local Law No.1 of the Year 1969 (JULY) Town of Wallkill, County of Orange, State of New York

A Local Law Regulating The Assembly of Persons in Public Places . . .

SECTION 1

This local law shall regulate the assembly of persons, where such assembly exceeds five thousand (5,000) persons, in public places within the Town of Wallkill.

SECTION 2.1 DEFINITIONS

ASSEMBLY shall mean the gathering, collecting, or congregating of persons with or without the levy of an admission fee.

PUBLIC PLACE shall mean a place to which the public or a substantial group of persons is invited or has access.

SECTION 3.1

No person shall use, allow, let or permit to be used property for the assembly of persons in excess of five thousand (5,000) unless a written permit authorizing such use shall have been obtained from the Town Board.

SECTION 3.2

Application for such permit shall be by verified petition. . . . Such application shall include the following written material:

k. A statement specifying whether any outdoor lights or signs are to be utilized. . . . In addition, no light on any part of property of assembly shall be permitted to shine beyond the property line of the property.

n. A statement that no soot, cinders, smoke, noxious acids, fumes, gases or disagreeable or unusual odors shall be permitted to emanate from the property so as to be detrimental to any person or to the public or which either annoys, disturbs, injures, endangers, or may have a tendency to annoy, disturb, injure or endanger the comfort, repose, health, peace or safety of any person or the public.

o. A statement that no music shall be played in any place of assembly, either by mechanical device or live performance, in such a manner that the sound emanating therefrom shall be audible beyond the property line of the place of assembly nor in a manner which either annoys, disturbs, injures, endangers, or tends to annoy, disturb, injure or endanger the comfort, repose, health, peace or safety of other persons or the public.

p. A statement that no loud, unnecessary or unusual noise shall be permitted to be made, continued or caused to be made or continued, which either annoys, disturbs, injures or endangers or tends to annoy, disturb, injure or endanger the comfort, repose, health, peace or safety of other persons or the public.

SECTION 3.3

The Town Board, before issuing any permit, shall require the approval of any or all of the following applicable governmental agencies:

a. The Orange County Health Department, the Town Sanitary Inspector, the Town Health Officer and the New York State Water Resources Commission as to any proposed sanitary sewage disposal system.

c. The Orange County Highway Department, the New York State Department of Transportation, the Orange County Sheriff's Department, the New York State Police, the Chief Engineer of the controlling Fire District, the Fire Commissioners of the controlling Fire District, and the Fire Advisory Board of the Town of Wallkill, as to the proposed parking area and the means of ingress and egress to such parking area.

d. The Zoning Board of Appeals and Building Inspector as to the proposed type, number and location of any sound producing equipment.

[Subsections b, e, f, g, h, i, and j refer respectively to approval of water supply, food and drink concessions and the disposal of the resulting refuse, security arrangements, fire protection, outdoor lights and signs, medical and nursing facilities, and camping or housing facilities.]

SECTION 3.4

b. No permit shall be issued unless the applicant shall furnish the Town with a comprehensive liability insurance policy insuring the Town against liability for damage to persons or property with limits of not less than $500,000.00–$1,000,000.00 for bodily injury or death and limits of not less than $500,000.00 for property damage. . . .

c. No permit shall be issued unless the applicant shall deposit with the Town Clerk cash or good surety company bond, approved by the Town Clerk, in the minimum sum of $100,000.00 and, in addition, the sum of $100,000.00 for each 5,000 persons in excess of 5,000 persons expected to attend the assembly for a maximum sum of $500,000.00. . . .

SECTION 3.5

The Town may deny issuance of a permit if it shall find that any of the items set forth in Section 3.2 of this local law are insufficient to properly safeguard the safety, health, welfare and well-being of persons or property or if the necessary approval of any governmental agency as set forth in Section 3.3 of this law is not obtained.

SECTION 3.6

If after the permit is issued, the Town Board through its lawful agents determines that any of the items set forth in Section 3.2 of this local law and as specified in the applicant's verified petition in support of the application for a permit is not adhered to and accomplished within a reasonable time of the date or dates set for the assembly through the time of the assembly, or if the necessary approval of any governmental agency as set forth in Section 3.3 of this local law is revoked at any time, such permit shall become null and void.

SECTION 6.1

Should any section or provision of this local law be decided by the courts to be unconstitutional or invalid, such decision shall not affect the validity of the local law as a whole or any part thereof other than the part so decided to be unconstitutional or invalid.

SECTION 7.1

This local law shall become effective after filing in the office of the Secretary of State, State of New York.

PROGRESS (?) REPORT: JULY 15

LAND: None

STAFF: Same as June, give or take twenty people. Fifty construction workers redundant

TICKET RECEIPTS: $537,123

TALENT BOOKINGS: Shaky

ATTORNEYS: One in New York City for Woodstock Ventures; one in New York City for film and record contracts; one in Wallkill for suing; one in New York City for political influence; one in Liberty, New York for land acquisition

PORTABLE TOILETS: Another additional 500 ordered, for a total of 2,000

MONEY SPENT: $481,519

MAKING WHITE LAKE

John on Max Yasgur and the New Site

It just wasn't gonna happen in the town of Wallkill, and by July 15 everybody but everybody knew it. With their customary graciousness, the Concerned Citizens called a press conference to celebrate our imminent departure and threw out a caveat to all of our ticket emptors to the effect that they should immediately seek refunds.

God will get them for that.

The wire services faithfully telegraphed this punch to our corporate breadbasket around the nation, and the New York office was suddenly transformed into a veritable hive of inactivity. Mail orders dwindled to a trickle and most of our ticket outlets announced that they would suspend all sales operations until they were satisfied that there was a site for the Festival.

Then the Attorney General's office called and inquired, with chilling politeness, as to the matter of our policy re: refunds. No policy at all, I informed the man. We've already got an alternate site lined up.

I was lying, of course, but that was July 15. The miracle of Woodstock—apart from the fact that Joel's acne cleared up—was that by July 16 I was almost telling the truth.

The wretched treatment we had suffered at the hands of the Wallkillians had not gone unnoticed, and fair-minded men all over the state began calling our office to commiserate with us. Amazingly enough, most of them just happened to know of a piece of land in their particular area that would suit our purposes perfectly. Theirs. We were offered riverfronts, mountainsides, wilderness areas, ski jumps, and even airstrips. One guy went so far as to suggest draining a fifty-acre lake on his property and selling it to us. "Make a real nice amphitheater." Another call came from a man who had vigorously opposed our presence on the Mills estate by arguing that we represented a threat to local life and morals and who now wanted to know whether we had at last come to our senses and made the decision to rent one of his extensive holdings. I thanked him for thinking of us and suggested that he go fuck himself. A moment after hanging up on him, I got *the* call.

It was Michael, announcing the existence of one Max Yasgur and some six hundred acres of dairy pasture in neighboring Sullivan County. Max, it turned out, had been following the events in Wallkill with growing dismay. An old-fashioned sort of fellow, he believed that you should not hate people just because they are different. He believed that even the lowest of God's creatures (hippies) should be accorded the same rights and privileges as non-Gentiles. He believed in the American Constitution and the right of peaceable assembly. He believed that Wallkill had done us wrong.

He also believed in money.

Accordingly, Michael had been invited to inspect his property, and if it met our requirements it was ours for the weekend of August 15 for a piddling $50,000 plus $75,000 in escrow to cover any damage that might occur. As land deals go, this one sounded like an insurance policy with the premium and the face value reversed, but it still looked more attractive than the prospect of $500,000 in refunds, so I told Michael to go ahead and look the property over. Several hours later he called back to tell me that the location was even better than Wallkill, that Max was a prince, that the local townspeople were already in love with us, and that I should be up there the next morning with our lawyers and some heavy bread.

We were off and running again.

With the help of our PR and legal staffs, Joel and I concocted an ad calculated to assure our prospective audience that the show would go on. It was a brilliant ad if I do say so myself, and we ran it for a week straight in every newspaper we could find:

TO INSURE THREE DAYS OF PEACE & MUSIC WE'VE LEFT WALLKILL AND ARE NOW AT WHITE LAKE, N.Y.*

Certain people of Wallkill decided to try to run us out of town before we even got there.

They were afraid.

Of what, we don't know.

We're not even sure that they know.

But anyway, to avoid a hassle, we moved our festival site to White Lake, Town of Bethel (Sullivan County), N.Y. We could have stayed, but we decided we'd rather switch now, and fight Wallkill later.

After all, the whole idea of the festival is to bring you three days of peace and music.

Not three days of dirty looks and cold shoulders.

Just one more word about those *concerned citizens* of Wallkill—

Our lawyers have been instructed to start damage proceedings immediately.

Now to something a bit more pleasant.

Our New Site.

It's twice the size of our original site. (Who knows, maybe the people of Wallkill did us a favor?) That means twice as many trees. And twice as much grass. And twice as many acres of land to roam around on.

For those of you who have already purchased tickets, don't

worry. Your tickets, even though printed Wallkill, will of course be accepted at our new festival site at White Lake in the Town of Bethel.

We'd also like at this time to thank the people of Bethel for receiving the news of our arrival so enthusiastically.

See you at White Lake, for the first aquarian exposition, Aug. 15, 16, and 17.

*White Lake, Town of Bethel, Sullivan County, N.Y.

WOODSTOCK MUSIC & ART FAIR

Having disposed of that, we turned our attention to calling performers and managers and telling them not to drop out, because the Festival was really "gonna go down." After considerable wrangling, they condescended to accept more money and perform at our new site. One or two acts even agreed to play for the originally negotiated fee.

The rest of the day was spent at the Bank hustling up two certified checks amounting to $125,000—a mere bagatelle. We then corralled our attorney, rented a car for the next morning, and plopped down for a few hours of edgy slumber.

The following day, forty miles down the Quickway, we turned off at the Monticello exit and followed Route 17B to the tiny hamlet of White Lake in the Town of Bethel, or whatever. There we obtained directions to the imposing establishment of Max Yasgur, dairy farmer extraordinaire, who was waiting for us on the front porch with his lawyer and his banker.

He was a tall lean man of about sixty with thinning gray hair and leathery skin. His surprisingly soft and innocent eyes had humor wrinkles around them and his voice was pleasantly deep and assured. He was a successful dairy farmer, I learned, with some prize bulls and about a thousand milk cows. He supplied a good part of Sullivan County with its milk, and despite the fact that he was Bethel's wealthiest resident, he was extremely well liked in the town. He was a man of influence and stature with a reputation for fair-minded shrewdness. He was Jewish; I liked him immediately.

I asked him how the town would feel about us coming up there and producing a rock festival that might attract as many as seventy-five thousand people. He told me that this part of Sullivan County had been dying for years. The tourist trade was going elsewhere. The hotels, stores, and restaurants around White Lake weren't doing good business any more. He felt that the Festival would be a big boost for local industry and maybe put the area on the map again. He was sure that the town would welcome us with open arms, and most of the people who would have any say in the matter were his friends anyway. Here Max's lawyer broke in to suggest that it really wasn't any of the town's business what Max did on his private property, especially for as short a period as three days. I answered that that was all very nice, but that our experience in Wallkill indicated that a town's concept of what its business was sometimes didn't square with that philosophy. Max then conceded that we would probably have to get certain permits from the town at some point, but he had taken the precaution of arranging a town meeting to deal with that eventuality, and it was scheduled for that very week.

This calmed my fears sufficiently for us to start wrestling about other issues. I said we had to build roads into the parking and camping areas. He frowned. I said we would take them out afterward. He smiled. He said that he couldn't spare the three-hundred or so extra acres we needed for parking and camping. I whimpered. He said some adjoining landowners would probably rent it to us. I cheesed.

Michael's people had told me pretty much everything that we'd require, so I was able to bargain with Max with some assurance. Price wasn't at issue; only the extent of the purchase, but Max proved to be an astute negotiator. He kept reminding me that we had no place else to go, and by way of response I kept rising from my chair with an air of indifference and walking meaningfully toward the door. I would pause at the threshold, toss a withering "Oh yeah?" over my shoulder, and then fall to my knees and beg Max to be reasonable. He would then refer irrelevantly to his recent heart attack and win his point.

And so it went, hour after hour. By the end of the afternoon, I had been bludgeoned—or coronaried—into total acquiescence, and Max and I shared a carton of chocolate milk while the attorneys retired to the den to draw up the papers. At 10:30 P.M. the deal was closed. Hands were shaken all around and the Woodstock contingent stumbled out into the night.

As we were driving toward New York, Michael Lang, as usual, had the final word. "You know," he said, "when we start working on that pasture up there, there'll be so much going on we'll lose track of the provisions of the contract that we've violated. Of course," he added after a considerable pause, "Max'll probably lose track, too."

We were running true to form.

Joel on Buying Off the Underground

I happened to be in Michael's office when the call came in from New York's radical underground. I listened in as he was invited to accompany his ass down to a meeting at an address in the East Village. Under discussion would be ways and means of averting several foreseen disasters associated with our impending "moth-ahfuggin' capitalist-hype-rip-off" festival.

"Far out!" said the ever-loquacious Michael as he hung up the phone.

"Yeah," I said, not really understanding what was going on. "What's with those guys anyway?"

"All kinds of bad shit, man. Free Festival riots. Busting up the performers' pavilion. Acid in the drinking water . . ."

"Acid! Whattaya mean, acid?" I was beginning to really understand what was going on.

"I mean acid, man. Sunshine. Fifty thousand kids on surprise trips."

"Mother-of-pearl! What the hell have those guys got against us? What do they want?"

"I don't know what they'll ask for, man. They're weird dudes. Could be anything. Free tickets, maybe, or a booth for their leaflets and shit. Fuck it! They may even want some stage time. All kinds of bummers."

I nodded, thinking for perhaps the twelfth time that week about the joys of a legal career.

The next day, Michael, Artie, and I trooped downtown. Our tumbrel deposited us in front of one of the seedier buildings in one of the seediest parts of the Village. We climbed the stoop and knocked. A shaggy preape opened the door and ushered us into a narrow murky hallway.

"Wait here," it said, turning and entering a room from which murmurs, shouts, and raucous laughter came in discomforting waves.

We stationed ourselves in some fold-up wooden chairs, awaiting our summons. Signs of strain proliferated. Artie, for example, took on the appearance of a cartoon rodent, eyes darting, mouth gibbering. I put an eyelock on the floor and listened to the low monotone that was issuing from behind Michael's Marlboro. It quickly got on my already abraded nerves.

"Michael?" I said, but there was no response, no break in the gnawing incantation, though we were sitting fringed elbow to fringed elbow.

"Michael!"

"What?" he said finally, from a great distance.

"What's that sound you're making?"

"What sound?"

"You're going m-m-m-m-m. Can't you hear yourself?"

"It's an OM, man. You know. A meditation chant." He resumed his droning and, in seconds, he was again as glazed as a jelly apple.

Another hoot of laughter came from behind the door, and I wondered what sort of thing such people would find amusing —a disturbing line of speculation. My stomach did an imitation of a granny knot.

Then the door opened and the same troglodyte as before beckoned us inside. There were about a dozen people scattered around the room on tables and chairs. They looked like vaguely bookish graduate students, although perhaps a little shaggier than average. No one had a bone in his nose. They were just guys like us.

All but one, that is; a massive German shepherd who took a sudden fancy to my throat when I advanced manfully to shake hands with the Leader. I should have noticed the dog. He was comparatively hairless and he was the only one in the room who wasn't wearing blue jeans.

"Down, Floyd!" said the chief heavy, known to the world as Abbie Hoffman.

Everyone laughed uproariously, not least of all my two partners, who took good care to synchronize their chuckles with Floyd's. So much for our united front.

"Well," I squeaked, "you gentlemen wanted to see us?"

It is difficult to sound confident and composed in the G clef. Artie tugged nervously on one of my fringes. Protocol apparently dictated that they make the opening statement.

"So," said Abbie in his best Schutzstaffel manner, "you guys are Woodstock Ventures, huh?" It was an editorial, not an inquiry. I got the feeling that he thought we were too innocuous to be producing a mothahfuggin' capitalist-hype etc.

"Well, look," he said, "you probably think we're out for publicity, right? Or that maybe we want to make converts. Well, you can put your minds at ease. It's nothing that complicated. All we want is $10,000, in cash."

The tiny spasm of relief that had accompanied his prefatory remarks drowned in a rising sea of bile.

"What?" I shrieked.

"Ten G's," he replied placidly. "Or Else."

"Or Else: what?" I said in a moronic show of truculence.

To do Abbie credit, he did not lack a sense of theater. He raised his fist high into the air and brought it down on the table with a crash that prompted Floyd to bare his fangs.

"Or Else—" meaningful pause—"that fucking festival you guys are planning is gonna end up around your ass."

This blatant threat brought all three of us—and Floyd—to our feet. Not to protest, mind you; but to flee.

"We'll be back to you," I said as we scraped and bowed our way jerkily toward the door.

And we were. We forked over a few thousand eventually, which ostensibly went for a couple of booths at the Festival for Panthers and other creatures of the forest. I look on it as money well spent. Not that the underground could have competed with all the unpremeditated disasters we experienced. It's just that their benign neglect of us was the only aspect of the whole Woodstock fiasco that cost less than was originally estimated.

John on the Hog Farm

One of Woodstock Venture's first employees was a fellow by the name of Stanley Goldstein. Having worked with Michael in Florida on a variety of projects, most notably the Miami Pops Festival, he was hired by us to serve as his all-purpose assistant, idea man, organizer, backup, and general factotum.

Stanley was an aging hippie, tall and thin, with longish hair and an impressive black beard. He had a world-weary and often cynical manner which implied that whatever you were planning, or said, or did, well, he had seen it all before and it would most likely turn out to be a colossal bummer. That mannerism aside, Stanley was competent, hard-working, articulate, and, alas, usually right. In bizarre contrast to his attitude of habitual pessimism was his almost manic enthusiasm for the plans and ideas which would occasionally erupt from his own perfervid brain. One such notion involved retaining the services of the Hog Farm.

The late sixties were the heydey of the dropout commune. The idea of getting it all together in some remote spot, getting back to the land, sharing equally with one's fellows, eschewing material gain, etc. had snared many young and many not so young peace-love-and-beauty seekers in this dawning of the Aquarian hype. Generally speaking, these communes were removed both physically and spiritually from the rest of the world, the idea being that they were It: not way stations, but final destinations. Exceptions to this rule were groups such as Ken Kesey's Merry Pranksters and the Hog Farm. Founded by serious thinkers, these communities were intended as genuine social experiments. They thrived on contact with the outside world, and sought to persuade and edify by their example.

Goldstein's idea, for which he lobbied fanatically, was to engage the Hog Farm for peace-keeping, medical, and general-assistance purposes. They had apparently rendered valuable services at other rock concerts, and their fee was simply transportation to and from the festival. Stanley argued persuasively that a peace-keeping force that looked, talked, and smelled like the crowd would be both highly credible and highly effective. He added that all Hog Farm members were experts on things like pitching tents, building fires, and tying knots, and thus could act as counselors to our many campers. Finally, and most important, they were wise in the ways of drugs, knowing good acid from bad, good trips from bummers, good medicine from poison, etc. Drugs, from the start, were one of our biggest worries, and the prospect of having seventy experienced paramedical personnel on hand was a comforting one. We were soon convinced; it made sense on all counts, and Stanley was dispatched to New Mexico's mountains, from whence our help was to come. To bring it where it would be needed, he chartered a Boeing 727, at a cost of some $17,000. It proved to be very well-spent money.

I first realized that the Hog Farm was among us when my father telephoned me on Thursday evening, August 7. He had seen a picture in the *Post* showing the arrival of the group at Kennedy: a lot of bizarre individuals standing around freaking out the travelers. The caption announced that they had come to serve as an auxiliary security force for the upcoming Woodstock Festival. What, my father wanted to know, had happened to the police? And we were out of our minds, etc., etc. SEVENTEEN THOUSAND DOLLARS!!?? I calmly told him that the operative word was auxiliary. They were just going to help out. As for the money, well, for reasons I was sure he wouldn't understand, the expense was fully justifiable, etc., etc., blah, blah, cringe.

The Hog Farm was trucked up to White Lake on August 9, and they set about earning their air fare in diverse and wonderful ways. They helped with the clearing and preparation of the camping areas. They lent their services to the completion of the stage. They bought huge quantities of rice—and later distributed it free to hungry kids. They established liaison with our Dr. William Abruzzi's medical force and trained volunteers to handle the anticipated bad drug trips.

The head Hog Farmer, High Romney, a.k.a. Wavy Gravy, a jovial toothless fellow, proved to be a superb organizer, crowd soother, and stage announcer. Once the Festival began, he spent most of his time on stage, calming the crowd when it rained and telling them how beautiful they all were when the vibes were otherwise bad. He also told jokes, fairy tales, and bedtime stories, holding that massive audience in the palm of his hand. To my mind he was the star of the show. He was invaluable.

On Saturday the drug problem started escalating. From the stage, Wavy Gravy started interspersing warnings about bad acid in his please-call-home announcements. His fellow Farmers co-operated with the medics and the State Police in trying to prevent bad trips and talk down those who had already departed on them. One unusual walkie-talkie broadcast I monitored at the old Telephone Building, which we had rented as a kind of off-site headquarters, was between a trooper near the stage and a Hog Farmer at the medical tent. The subject was good and bad acid, and the trooper's question was how to tell them apart.

"Think of it this way, man: good acid is green; bad acid is blue."

"O.K. Let me be sure I've got this right. The good acid is the green acid and the bad acid is the blue acid."

"That's it, man. Good, green. Bad, blue. Ya got it?"

"Yeah, I think so. Good, green. Bad, blue. Right?"

"Right on!"

"Thanks."

Only in America.

When the Festival ended, the Hog Farmers stayed behind to organize the cleanup volunteers. On August 22, they headed back to New Mexico. On all fronts and in all respects they had done more than they'd been asked to—and probably more to generate the famous Woodstock good vibes than anybody else. I don't recommend their company to anyone who aspires to be a cynic.

Joel on Haw-riss

The bug-eyed creature with the Brooklyn accent who stood before me outside the production trailer contrasted sharply with the air and the trees and the sky. This was the Catskills, though, and he was by no means the only sharpie in the immediate area. A few minutes earlier, for example, our own corporate specimen had asked me to step outside and deal with him.

"Michael, how can I deal with him? I don't even know what he's doing here."

"Oh yeah. Sorry, man. Thing is, he's very heavy in the town. Like he got the racetrack put in when the people were against it. We need him to keep things cool with the locals."

"Do you know this for sure? I mean, have you checked him out or anything?"

"Oh sure, man. It's cool. Look, I had a check made up for $2,500. He wants $10,000 for the whole gig, but I don't want to give it to him in advance."

"Look, Michael, if you've been dealing with him so far, maybe you'd . . ."

"Don't sweat it, Joel," he interrupted, flashing a smile that filled me with misgivings. By now I was constantly on the lookout for the one encounter with Lang that would result in my going to prison. A few minutes later, however, I was nose to nose with this Horace person, who was telling me how he had helped "a certain party" get a "certain referendum" passed. Horace was sure that he could be of similar assistance to us.

Now this was big-time corporate stuff. Woodstock Ventures, on the threshold of greatness, was about to hire its very own lobbyist. No Dita Beard, perhaps, but a real live lobbyist nonetheless. As in a vision, I pictured Horace gliding through State House cloakrooms, arm in arm with senators and assemblymen, chatting wittily of Woodstock. One of the legislators picks up a phone and calls the ringleader of the Stop-the-Festival gang. The legislator smiles, hangs up, and rejoins our lobbyist. . . .

What could be more civilized?

Horace could, for openers. Those three D's that are the hallmark of a gentleman—Dress, Demeanor, and Diction—had been hiding behind some other part of the alphabet when the Lord made Horace. In addition to being slovenly and inarticulate, he bore an unnerving resemblance to a frog. I wondered if there were any frogs in Brooklyn.

My public-relations effort desperately needed a shot in the arm. I wanted the town to love us the way we deserved to be loved. And yet somehow the thought of love seemed incompatible with the good offices of a person like Horace. Horace was greedy, for example. He wanted the whole ten grand up front.

"Jo-well, ya gotta unnerstan'. I got expenses, Jo-well."

This overarticulated rendering of my name, starting and concluding each of his ejaculations, left me wishing my parents had called me Burt.

"Now Haw-riss," I said, hoping I would sound more persuasive if I spoke to him in his native dialect, "ya gotta unnerstan' that no businessman in his right mind would pay the entire amount up front. We gotta see results, Haw-riss."

I remember thinking at that moment that I had no idea what "results" should look like. An absence of massed pitchforks, maybe? No sudden jump in the sales of pillows and tar? Discounts for our employees at the local stores?

"Jo-well, you're da bawss, Jo-well."

Gracious to a fault, even as he conceded his point, Horace pocketed the check and lumbered back toward his dusty sedan.

Could *that* make *them* love *us?* Maybe, using Big Brother's methods.

He must have sensed my doubts, because he turned as he got to his car and waved the $2,500 in my direction.

"Just let 'em give me any trouble, Jo-well. Just let 'em." His voice became—impossibly enough—hoarser. "I'll ram this Festival down their fucking throats."

An odd prelude to three days of Peace and Music. What the hell was I doing giving money to such a man?

The negotiations had taken ten minutes. In that time, we had gone from loather and loathee dickerers to loather and loathee business associates, an unedifying progression no matter how you look at it. I was even supposed to write up a contract based on our discussion, to be signed at a later date. There turned out to be no need for such a document, however, because less than a week later our image in White Lake really went to hell.

Joel on the Earthlite Theatre

The tale of the Earthlite Theatre was told to me one dark and dreary August evening by Don Ganoung, a man of the cloth skilled in working with Jews and Gentiles alike. He had been assigned the task of seeing to it that we didn't make the same mistakes in White Lake that had gotten us kicked out of Wallkill, and he accomplished that task magnificently.

We made different mistakes.

At first everything had gone well. Under Woodstock's and Ganoung's auspices, a new Little League team had come into existence, a new Sunday-school course taught by the Rev. D. Ganoung himself had begun to enliven White Lake's houses of worship, a spate of afternoon teas had helped calm the breasts of suspicious mothers, and a number of well-planned chance encounters between local citizens and "selected" Woodstock staffers had laid the groundwork for enduring coexistence. Unselected employees had been banned from walking the streets in daylight. Only Max was exposed to them, and if they got his dander up, he had only to consult his bulging bank balance to get his dander right back down again. All was peace and light.

Then the Earthlite struck.

By the late sixties, an unappetizing art form known as "street theater" had emerged. In sidewalk restaurants all over America, lunches turned sour as ragged bands of thespians mimed the destruction of the Establishment and strong-armed alfresco diners into participating. Every now and then, one of these troupes would gain a fragile permanence, usually as a result of having maintained the same cast for more than seven days, and in extremely rare cases they might even be lucky enough to be hired to perform on an honest-to-goodness stage. Thus, when the Earthlite Theatre was invited to stride the boards at the El Monaco Motel, White Lake, New York, they nearly trampled each other in their eagerness to accept. To be sure, the El Monaco was not the Copacabana and the pay wasn't much more than a dollar fifty above room and board, but it sure beat the Sheep Meadow in Central Park.

What El Monaco's proprietor saw in the Earthlite people is something of a mystery. Perhaps he felt there was an untapped market for their sort of thing. Where, he probably queried, can the avant-garde in this area go to be amused at night? What avant-garde? he neglected to query.

Meanwhile, despite all his teas and kiddy sermons, Don Ganoung was beginning to pick up rumbles of a stop-the-Festival movement. He made inquiries and was told that, while his contributions to the community were certainly appreciated, appreciation alone was not going to get him very far. Parents and landowners were afraid, he discovered. Not because of anything we'd done, but because of everything we planned to do. The people of White Lake were nervous about our Festival, poor sillies. What happens, they wanted to know, when tens of thousands of screaming hippies crest yonder ridge where Grandpa Van Amerongen first broke the earth back in neolithic times? What happens when scores of drugged rock stars take to the stage with their godless music?

Simple fear of the unknown was Ganoung's diagnosis. His antidote: make the unknown familiar. Have a pre-Festival festival.

Good old Don. I can never think of him without smiling inwardly as my fingernails dig into the flesh of my palms. In fairness, though, it was really a good idea: two or three sanitized acts performing before four or five dozen hand-picked sanitized long-hairs. The locals couldn't help but be pacified.

White Lake's Concerned Citizens Committee was gaining momentum every day, so there wasn't a moment to lose. Michael gave Don the O.K., and preparations for the prefestival began immediately. Arranging for a presentable audience was easy. The staff at the site together with the sons and daughters of the Concerned would do nicely. The entertainment was another matter.

Being frugal with his employer's money—a trait which very nearly disqualified him from working for us—Ganoung set about securing the cheapest talent available. For openers, he persuaded some of our construction workers, who had a fledgling rock band, to lead off the bill. Then he got bogged down. It appeared that nobody else wanted to perform at his outing. Certainly none of the acts that had been hired for the Festival proper was prepared to come up a week early and play for pennies. In fact, every group Don talked to, famous or obscure, felt that the whole gig was just too demeaning to bother with, not to mention risky. It was perfect for the Earthlite.

At the time, the Theatre was not exactly packing them in over at the El Monaco, but since they had insisted on a long-term contract before consenting to cast their pearly talents before swinish upstaters, the empty tables were more a threat to ego than to job security. Still, the status of ego in show business is such that, by the time Ganoung approached the Earthliters with his little project, they were ready to perform before an open stall in the men's room just to be sure of an audience. Thus, haggling was kept to a minimum, and the following bargain was struck: the troupe would do its act, and the attendant publicity would be its compensation.

A clear case of pennywise and pound foolish.

For the next few days, Don felt like quite a big-time producer. He prepared a portion of the site for his opening and anxiously searched the skies for omens of good weather. Just like a producer, he checked and double-checked the readiness of his sound equipment and his stage crew. When word filtered in that the number of townspeople attending would be huge, he was delighted. The night before the show he had trouble getting to sleep.

Thursday, August 7, was clear and warm. Around 2:00 P.M., almost exactly on schedule, the Reverend reached for the center-stage mike and welcomed a somewhat hostile crowd of several hundred to the Woodstock nation. He was brief and, he hoped, winning. He said that everything the audience was about to see would be both representative and entertaining. Then he left the stage and bade the games begin.

The construction-crew rock group did well, considering the distraction of playing to an audience with its hands over its ears. The Earthlite contingent would have done well, too, if only the hands had been moved to the eyes. Their first skit was about weather gods or some such thing. It was funny and a good crowd-warmer. But with "attendant publicity" the troupe's only compensation, they made sure that their second skit was more memorable.

They commenced to strip.

As they got down to bare pimples, they began to hurl nasty alliterations at the audience.

"Repressed rednecks!" they shouted, and the last few garments joined a pile of clothes at the side of the stage.

Then, the Earthlite was unconditionally naked.

"Provincial prudes!" they screamed to a momentarily paralyzed audience. "Loosen the chains and live!" With that, the players fell upon one another in a riveting facsimile of an orgy.

The crowd response was electric. Children rushing forward to get a better view were intercepted by parents who had seen that sort of thing before, in *The Ten Commandments,* and knew that it was a no-no. Cars by the dozen with curious young noses pressed against the rear windows careened out of sight in the exodus back to God's country, and Ganoung was left to sift among the ruins of his community-relations program.

Later, in rump session—and I use the term nervously—over at Andy's Bar and Grill, the citizens of White Lake got together and voted to have a full town meeting the following night. The agenda: Stop Woodstock.

COUNTDOWN

John on John's Sunday

It was Sunday, August 10, 1969. I was sitting in our apartment and the phone was ringing. The calls were business calls, and they were driving me up the chimney, or the walls, or a tree, or what-have-you. The Festival, it seemed, was running into a few snags after we'd spent a couple of million on it. We still weren't too sure where we were going to hold it, for example, and some of our performers were getting cold feet. The stage wasn't finished and the fences weren't up. The food hadn't arrived yet either, but that was O.K., because the food stands still weren't built. Everything was slated to kick off in five days, and that's why the phones were ringing. I was answering them because it was my money.

At about eleven o'clock, I snapped. An occasional hysterical phone call is one thing. An unrelieved procession is another. Besides, I didn't have the answers. In most cases, I didn't even understand the questions. So I decided that the best thing to do was get the hell out of the apartment and go somewhere I couldn't be reached. It was a really pretty morning and I headed for Central Park to get in a few hours of sun. But when I got there I discovered I have this thing about watching happy and carefree New Yorkers (compared to me, anyway) gambol in the park when I feel like shit. It makes me edgy. Those people were making me think weird thoughts with their laughing and kids and dogs and bicycles. So I decided to go somewhere else.

My father has an apartment in the United Nations Plaza building which he uses during the week. On weekends it's empty. When I first came to the big city to lose my fortune, I stayed there for a while, and as I do with hotels, I kept the key after I left. It still dangles from my key chain, wherever that is. Well, this old haunt of mine seemed like the perfect spot to spend the rest of the afternoon. Leaving the park, I hopped a cab at Fifth and 79th and sped downtown. The ride was uneventful except for an advertisement on WABC that promised three days of Peace and Music in White Lake, New York. My cabbie kept punctuating the message with little snarls of "fucking longhairs," suggesting the possibility of his nonattendance. Somehow I stifled the urge to tell him it was my festival they were touting and, instead, made him change a twenty for my $1.30 fare.

The U.N. Plaza building is one of New York's prestige residences. The roster of tenants includes some of the wealthiest and most prominent citizens of our burg, and they are more than faithfully guarded by the building staff. As I entered the front door, dressed Sunday casual, I was greeted affably thus: "Deliveries round the back, bub."

"My father lives here," I replied.

"Yeah? What's his name?" the doorman retorted.

"Alfred Roberts," I said.

"What apartment?" he said.

"Fourteen E," I said.

"Wrong," he said. "It's fourteen D."

"Oh well, look, D, E, what's the difference? It's easy to forget those things."

"Not if you're his son, it isn't," he said. "Look, you got any identification on you?"

"No, but I can describe the inside of the apartment for you if you want."

"Maybe you delivered there before. How the hell do I know?"

"Look here," I said, "you may be making a terrible mistake as far as your future career is concerned. Now let me the hell upstairs."

That seemed to decide him and he turned resignedly to the desk man behind him. "Louie," he said, "call the police."

"Wait a second," I said. "That was a little hasty of me, but there's no need to call the cops. I know my father has a picture of me in the living room. Why don't you come upstairs with me, look at the picture, and if it's me, let me stay?"

Miraculously, Louie continued to dial. I walked over to the phone and put my finger down on the button.

"Hey!" yelled Louie. "What you think you're doing?"

"You win," I said. "You figured me out. I'm a fourteenth-story man. I'll make you a little deal. You let me upstairs into old man Roberts' apartment and I'll split with you. But if I don't pinch anything, like if I'm not in the mood, then you get nothing. How am I doing?"

"Hey, Bill," said the desk man, "we got us a comedian. Look, buddy, I don't know you from Adam. You got no ID and the apartment is empty. Now what do you want me to do?"

"I have one final suggestion," I said. "Call my father in New Jersey. He may be at home. Ask him to describe me, or, even better, let me talk to him. You can listen in. How's that?"

He shrugged, opened a large black book, and actually did it. When my father answered the phone, he put me on.

"Hi, Dad," I said. "I'm trying to get upstairs into your apartment and the doorman doesn't believe I'm your son, so he's listening in."

My father is an occasional practical joker. "Exactly who is this?" he said.

"Come on, Dad. Give me a break," I pleaded. "I'm having a bad day."

"All right, Jock," he said. "Don't mess the place up."

And with that he hung up. The desk man nodded at the doorman, who gave a thumbs-up sign to the elevator man, and I proceeded to the fourteenth floor at long last.

I sat up there for a while and this strange malaise came over me. I have an odd psychological quirk. I like to hurt myself. If, for instance, I injure my finger or stub my toe or bite my tongue, I like to play with the injured part and make it hurt more. I can't leave it alone. Little physical pitfalls are my playthings. So instead of healing in a day or two, one of my toes can remain stubbed for a week. I'm not looking for sympathy. I just enjoy abusing my body in small ways. I court petty aggravations.

To bring this thought home, I was uneasy because the phone wasn't ringing and I didn't know what the hell was going on with the Festival. There was nothing I could do, but the need to know was all-powerful. I like to hear about disasters as they're occurring.

The silence in my father's apartment unnerved me and I bit my tongue. I always tie my stuff together like that. Then I picked up the phone and negated all the effort of the morning. I called my answering service and told them that if there were any more calls, I could be reached at my father's number. To emphasize my message, I gave them my father's number. After patiently taking my message, the answering-service lady confirmed my faith in the constancy of the universe by asking me who I was and then disconnecting before I could frame an answer she would understand. The thing was, even after four years as my answering service, she still didn't quite believe that my name was John. Those foolish enough to ask for me by that name were usually told that they had dialed a wrong number. Ask for Pierrot or Nguyen or something and I would get the message, usually in the following manner: "Any messages today, Gladys?" "Yes, I think so, Mr. R. It's a little tough to read, but I think it says, 'Gliok called and said . . .' and this part I can't make out. But I see here at the end it says—and Alice underlined this, Mr. R.—'Very Important.'" Today was no exception. In the fullness of time I managed to get her straight that I wanted all calls to be referred to me, John Roberts, at my father's number, where I would be until further notice. Several minutes later, I received the phone call that could have changed my life in a most agreeable fashion—but didn't.

Several weeks earlier, Woodstock Ventures had concluded a deal with two young film makers named Mike Wadleigh and Bob Meurice to make a movie of the Festival. The deal had been quite simple. They would raise all necessary monies, estimated to be about $100,000, for the production of the film. They would handle all distribution arrangements and would be given exclusive filming rights. In return, we would take fifty percent of the producers' fee after the distributor—whoever he was —got his cut. Wadleigh-Meurice would get thirty percent of our fifty percent. Simple enough. The problem was to find a distributor who would take a $100,000 fling for fifty percent of a movie about a festival that might not happen in a week. This was the meat of the telephone call I got from Bob Meurice that afternoon. They had been all over the place and no one wanted to put up the money. He was calling to find out if Woodstock would put up the necessary funds and thereby take one hundred percent instead of fifty percent.

If I ever have a nightmare—while I'm sleeping—you can be damn sure that my reply to that question will be in it. If memory serves, I said, "Look, Bob, this film thing is a risky affair at best. You guys have no real track record. The Festival may be a real dud cinematically speaking. We at Woodstock have made some fairly foolish expenditures over the last few months, but this is really out of the question. It's pie in the sky." I think I went into some theories of venture capital at that point, using words like high risk and low yield, etc.; all too painful to reconstruct. Then I said, "If there's one thing I know about documentaries, it's that they never ever make money. So, Bob, we're just going to pass on this one. But if there's anything I can do to help you get a distributor before Friday, just say the word. And, Bob, please. Whatever you do, don't put any of your own money into this kind of project."

I persuaded him, and the full measure of his gratitude can be known by revealing that the film that Warner Brothers eventually paid $100,000 for has grossed in the neighborhood of $17,000,000 at last count.

Nothing like a Sunday in August for doing business.

Joel on Mike in the Movies

On Monday, August 11, Jock and I were at Paul Marshall's office haggling with the food concessionaires when Paul's secretary put through a call to me from Our Man at the Site, the mostly Reverend Don Ganoung.

"It's happening *again*, Joel," said Ganoung in that resonant bass voice of his that always managed to inspire uneasiness.

"What's *it*?" I asked, running through a mental list of pending catastrophes.

"The town," he said. "They don't like us here any more."

(This was before I had heard about the Earthlite Follies.)

He sounded like a wounded child, and I sought to comfort him in his anguish. "What the hell are you talking about, Ganoung? Just five days ago you told me we could elect Michael mayor of White Lake if we wanted to. What the fuck's going on up there? I thought you were gonna teach Sunday school. I thought . . ." Remembering suddenly that I wasn't alone in the office, I tried to get a grip on myself. "O.K., Don. Just tell me what you think our status is now."

"That's just it, Joel. I'm not exactly sure. This morning I heard that there's going to be a town meeting tonight to consider the proposition of the Festival and . . ."

"Proposition of the Festival! What the hell does that mean? The Town Board approved the goddamn Festival last month!"

"Look, Joel, all I can tell you is what Amatucci [the Town Supervisor] told me. He says there's nothing to worry about, but I don't like the sound of it."

He doesn't like the sound of it. Jesus!

"What's Michael's reading of this?" I asked, afraid of the answer.

"Well, uh, that's sort of why I'm calling. I tried to get hold of Michael, but Ticia didn't know where he was. So I took the liberty of calling you directly."

This implicit apology for bypassing his boss irritated me, but, knowing Michael, I had to admit it had taken some nerve.

"Well, Don, I'm really glad you decided to call, even

though I don't sound like it. See what you can find out about this meeting tonight, and we'll get to work right away on our end. Somebody will either call you or be up there by midafternoon. And, Don, I'm sorry I got steamed up."

"Hey, that's O.K., Joel. I'll do some snooping. See ya."

Moments later, Jock and I sort of drew straws to see who would go careening up to Sullivan County to derive calm from calamity. I lost. Three hours later, I arrived in White Lake, full of dread.

The area that served as an anteroom for Michael's office at the Telephone Building had taken on a depressing resemblance to a Motor Vehicle Bureau office on renewal deadline day. Eight or ten construction-boss types in various states of impatience made a formless queue that seemed well on its way to becoming fossilized. Worrying needlessly about incurring displeasure by barging ahead, I strode into the back office proper, surprising no one except the lone Ticia, Michael's gopher. She had seen the look on my face before.

"Hi, Ticia. Where's Michael? And who are all those people outside?"

"Oh, them," she stammered. "Just some contractors."

"Just some contractors," I repeated numbly. "What are they waiting for? Payment?"

"Oh no. They just need Michael's O.K. on some plans."

"Well, how long have they been waiting?" I said. Something was beginning to throb in the vicinity of my left temple.

"Oh, uh, I dunno. I've been in and out all day."

The throbbing increased.

"Well, where the hell is Michael? Has he been in at all?"

"Of course he has."

"When, Ticia?"

"Look, I just told you. I've been in and out all day. I don't remember exactly when Michael was here and when he wasn't."

I began to get the feeling that I had pushed Michael's loyal servant as far as I could, and a plan hatched itself in my left temple while the throbbing obligingly made the trek over to my right temple to give it room.

"O.K., Ticia," I said as calmly as I could. "When he comes back, have him give me a call, will you?"

She nodded.

"You sure you don't know where he is?"

"No, I don't," she lied.

"O.K.," I lied back, "I'll be over at the motel."

I went through that grim waiting room and out into the bright Catskill sunlight where my car was parked. Whoever ordains the weather was offering me a sun-drenched afternoon that begged to be enjoyed. To cruise, free from corporate intrigue, through the lovely hills around White Lake tempted me much more than the scheme I was about to put into motion.

At the end of the block I made a right, then a U turn. Then I pulled off the road and waited.

If this had been a movie, the girl playing Ticia would have come scurrying out of the building a minute or two after whoever was playing me (Clint Eastwood) had left. Did that sort of thing happen in real life, or, if not in real life, in the kind of life I was living? It did indeed.

Right on cue, the door of the Telephone Building opened and out she raced, red hair trailing stiffly as she made for her car. She paused as she was about to climb in and looked up the block directly at the trees behind which my heart was thudding. But she didn't see me; in a flash she was in the car and using up a good deal of tire rubber as she accelerated toward the site. I followed at a discreet distance.

I pulled around a curve just short of the site and saw her car parked beyond the performance area where the road bordered on some rolling fields that Max had reserved for his unsuspecting cows. As I sped along that last quarter-mile, she jumped out of the car and loped toward the center of the pasture. I got the feeling that there was pay dirt beyond that first hill.

I was just a few steps behind her as she topped the rise. Some sixth sense told her that I was there, and she took two last strides and yelled, "Michael!" Before she could shout again, I had topped the rise myself to discover that Michael hadn't heard her.

He was too busy.

Every now and then, during the course of the frenetic over-purchasing of equipment that went on prior to the Festival, the record of a particularly insane acquisition would catch my eye. "Two Amphibious Ducks, unit cost $1200.00: $2400.00" was one such. When I had questioned that lulu, I had been informed that these vehicles were of the swamp-buggy genus and necessary for the reconnaissance of the marshier areas of our site. Standing next to Ticia, silent on a peak in the Borscht Belt, I got my first look at what our money had wrought.

I had no trouble locating it. In the middle of a large open field it resembled a huge orange beetle zipping back and forth at breakneck speed under the guidance of someone who apparently had had a lot of experience riding insects. He was a male, Caucasian, of medium build, sporting an impressive shrubbery of curly brown hair. Truth to tell, he was my partner, M. (nmn) Lang, Director of Production and Construction at the Woodstock Festival's White Lake site.

"It's finally happened," I said to myself. "He's gone completely bananas."

As if to confirm the thought, Michael waved cheerfully, steering for a moment with one hand.

"Forgive him for he knows not what he does," I intoned.

Then I saw the cameras.

Anyone could have missed them, given the activity at center stage. There was a crew of three: a cameraman glued to the back of an Arriflex, a sound man complete with a microphone and sound-gathering cone, and one of those ever-present assistants. I let my eyes wobble to a distant corner of the field where I noticed several other means of conveyance, to wit: a motorcycle, a large tractor, and a horse with a western saddle.

Ticia and I were on the set, watching a scene from "Michael Rides Again," Take Four.

Although I am known to my friends as being slow to anger, I set some kind of a speed record reaching a state that made apoplexy look like a coma. I had seen enough. A thousand popping blood vessels called on me to act, to strangle, to maim, to annihilate. The next thing I knew, I was racing down the hill toward the center of the field. That's when Michael realized it was me.

He drove over to me in his duck, stopping a prudent ten feet away, and smiled.

"Hey, man. What's happenin'?" was his greeting.

"What's happening? What's happening?" I couldn't seem to get my voice up to an audible level. I took a quick gulp of air. "What's happening, you miserable cocksucker"—now *there* was the voice—"is that the entire fucking work force is fucking waiting for you in your fucking office, you fucking sonofabitch!"

Dimly aware that I had been bobbing forward with each word, I tried to steady myself, and continued, "They . . . they're waiting f-f-f-for *you*, you slithering asshole, and you're out in a goddamn field making a . . . a . . . a . . ."

"A movie," Ticia prompted.

"Thank you. A movie." It seemed that what I had lost on the bobs I had made up on the stutters.

"Hey, man. It's just some promotional stuff. Take it easy," Michael said nervously. Second only to seeing him dismembered was seeing him frightened.

Ticia did some more prompting. "Some contractors are at the office, Michael. I told them you'd be right back."

It was slender, but Michael grabbed it.

"Far out, Tish. I'm on my way." He turned toward the camera crew. "Thanks a lot, guys. Get this stuff over to the shed, will you?"

Then, eschewing further chat, my partner sprang from his duck, bounded past the tractor and the horse, mounted the motorcycle, and rode off into the sunset.

I turned toward Ticia, who had some trouble meeting my gaze.

"Nice try, Tish," I said.

"Thanks, Joel. I'm sorry. I just want it to be over."

"Me, too, kiddo. Me, too."

Joel on Filippini's Farm

As soon as I got myself established up at the Festival site, I went around with the Rev. Don Ganoung to persuade all the owners of adjacent land that it would be the better part of valor for them to rent us their fields for a certain imminent three-day period. We knew it was unlikely that our audience would pay much attention to No Trespassing signs, so we offered the soon-to-be-besieged local farmers fantastic insurance coverage and a bona fide cleanup campaign in the hopes of heading off a spate of lawsuits in advance.

Before too long I found myself on the twenty-five-acre estate of one William Filippini. If ever there was a plot of land that was going to be overrun by our imported locusts, this was it. But Mr. Filippini didn't see it that way. He didn't quite get the concept of so many people. "Won't you have a little Chianti, and we'll talk about why I'm not going to rent you my property."

We sat down in his dining room, the Rev. Don Ganoung and I, and I could tell right away that Filippini didn't think that Don was truly a man of the cloth; certainly not a priest, in any event. He talked about the old country and how the Filippinis had come here and how he had worked very hard to get where he was in the farm community. There was just a hint of deferential resentment toward Max and the other local agricultural moguls in his voice. He wondered aloud about how Max could have extended such an invitation to catastrophe. Not that he had anything against *Mister* Ganoung or me—and that Michael was certainly a nice-enough boy except for his appearance—but it seemed odd; with all the farm land in the northeast to choose from, why had we chosen White Lake?

Mrs. Filippini didn't say a word for most of the conversation, but I got the feeling that she appreciated the situation better than her husband. She had spent some time around teen-agers and knew that the time to be compensated for their various atrocities and depredations was before they took place.

Finally Mr. Filippini allowed as how he would give some thought to the possibility of renting us the south ten acres that he hadn't been doing much with anyway. And if some people wanted to camp there, well, that was O.K. so long as they didn't bust anything up and they behaved themselves. I hesitated to say once again that, with thousands of kids in the area, he would be lucky to have the very structure of his house to himself, let alone his upper fifteen acres and his barn and his chicken coop.

I loved this Mr. Filippini. He was a little slow of thought but very well-meaning and much more honest than most of the people we had to deal with. I wanted to see him come out all right on this one. But I had dealt with stubborn farmers in the past. There was only so much talking I could do before his type stopped listening. I hoped for his sake that he would get a piece of the Woodstock parking-lot-and-campsite budget. His friends and neighbors were certainly planning to; whether because they couldn't dream of fighting such awesome numbers or because they didn't have any idea of what they were getting themselves into is an open question.

After much deliberation, a few more visits from the Reverend and myself, and a few more glasses of Chianti, Mr. Filippini decided at last to rent us a discrete portion of his land for a certain sum for a precise period of time. I was somewhat happier than I would have been with an outright refusal and drew up the papers on the spot. It was Thursday, the 14th.

Within twenty-four hours the levee had given way and every square inch of the poor man's property was awash with long-hairs. They were in the barn, burning the hay, trampling the alfalfa, freaking out the chickens, and cheerfully terrorizing the entire Filippini family. Responding to some primitive survival instinct, Mr. Filippini assembled his entire clan in the house. All his children and their families were crowded in. From time to time I would receive a frantic phone call from him, informing me that certain people were trespassing on parts of his land that Woodstock Ventures, Incorporated had not rented. I tried to be as understanding as I could about his anxiety in the midst of all the bedlam, but I ignored his demands that the police be called in to put the invaders to flight.

Once or twice, having made the perilous journey to the

performance area, I continued beyond it to see how Filippini was doing. There would always be a sentry in one of the upstairs windows, usually one of the grandchildren, who would immediately signal down to Granpa, sitting vigilant on the porch with a shotgun across his lap. Filippini honestly believed that a horde of drug-crazed hippies might charge the house, and he planned to take a few of them with him before he and his family went under.

During my visits, however, Filippini became the soul of hospitality, even if he was running a bit low on Chianti. As always, he would courteously request that we keep our patrons off the unrented portions of his demesne. Just as courteously, I would disclaim any responsibility for their being there in the first place.

In the end, despite everything, Mr. Filippini endured. He got $2,500 for allowing the kids onto a part of his land that they were going to overrun anyway. To repay him for all the good red wine he'd decanted for us, we extended our cleanup effort to include every single acre of his property. Only his chickens failed to recover fully from the trauma of the Festival, but those that didn't overdose now lay some of Sullivan County's most sought-after eggs.

Building Permits

Bethel, New York, outside the Town Hall
Tuesday, August 12, 1969, 4:05 P.M.

Joel is staring in disbelief at Don, the town Building Inspector, who is looking fixedly at the ground, his hands jammed into the back pockets of his jeans.

"You can't be serious," Joel says.

The Building Inspector shakes his head. "I'm only telling you what they told me."

"What they *told* you, for Christ's sake! Those permits have been authorized in writing!"

"Yes, they've been authorized. But they haven't been issued. Technically speaking, you're in violation right now."

Joel shuts his eyes and takes a deep breath. "Oh, come *on*, Don. Jesus! You and the board knew damn well we had to start building immediately if we were going to get ready in time. You telling me they authorized the permits so we could sit around doing nothing for three weeks?"

"No," says Don softly.

"Don't you see what they're doing, goddammit. They've got cold feet. They're welshing."

Don nods his head in agreement. "I know that. I know they authorized the permits. But now they're telling me not to issue them. So what the hell do I do?"

Joel regards him steadily. "Well, there are a couple of things I can say about that. First of all, when permits are authorized, they're supposed to be issued. You're legally obligated to issue them, and if you don't, well, you're acting outside the law. So that's one thing. The second thing is that if you go along with the board, you can be damn sure that we'll take both of you to court to recover damages, which figure to run into seven figures. Thirdly—and this may sound corny—but I think you've got a moral duty to issue those permits. They've been issued and nobody's withdrawn the authorization."

Don rocks back and forth from his toes to his heels and continues to stare at the ground. "Shit!" he says.

"That's what I say, too," Joel responds bitterly.

"I don't know what to do. I really don't."

"You don't know what to do! Well, shit, man; use your head. Those bastards in there are all sitting back nice and comfortable while you're standing out here catching all the flak. Don't you get the picture? They won't even put it in writing. They're making you the fall guy. They're afraid to go back on their word and they're afraid to authorize the Festival. So they tell you not to issue the permits, and you're left holding the bag, and we're out a couple of million dollars."

Don has stopped rocking. He stands silent, thinking.

"They're screwing us to the wall, Don, and they're gutless and underhanded enough to try to pass the buck. Don't let them get away with that, please."

Don lifts his eyes. "I'm giving you those permits."

Joel lets out his breath. "Thank you."

"When do you want them?"

"Any time during the next thirty seconds'll be fine."

They both laugh and turn to enter the Town Hall. Don heads for his office and Joel heads for a pay phone.

"Hello, Michael? This is Joel. Listen, I've got the permits. . . . Yeah, it is far out. Look, get hold of some transportation and get right down here. I'm gonna make copies and then you and me is gonna do a little postin'."

Fifteen minutes later, Joel is standing outside impatiently scanning the street for a sign of Lang. Then he notices a familiar-looking chestnut approaching at an easy canter. Michael is in the saddle.

"Joel!" he yells exultantly.

"Michael! What the hell . . ."

"If you got the permits, man, I got the transportation. Hop on."

For a moment Joel stands contemplating this *coup de théâtre*. Then he laughs and shakes his head. "You are a clown, Michael. You'll be the death of me yet."

Michael just smiles as Joel grasps his extended hand and climbs aboard. He has heard such things before.

John on a Visit to the Site

August 13 stands out in my mind as the absolute nadir in my relationship with my family on the subject of Woodstock. Before that day, my father had been all hopeful pessimism, my brother Billy all guarded optimism, and my brother Keith all undifferentiated disapproval. After that day, all three of them were galvanized into the frantic rescue job I mentioned earlier in the book. On that day, however, things could have gone either way, and everything hung in the balance . . . by the neck until dead.

For thirty days and thirty nights we had labored through wind and rain to prepare the White Lake site for the Festival. I had been to see it only twice, but with the certainty of an infant

I never doubted that it would be ready in time. Then, on the 12th, Joel called me and reported that work was going slowly, that he was not getting maximum co-operation from the staff, that it would be nip and tuck, etc. My original plans had involved my wrapping up ticket operations in New York on the 14th and moving them to White Lake the same day. Joel thought it might be a good idea for me to come up sooner, and on reflection I had to agree with him. Nip and tuck, after all, was not a phrase one used when discussing finishing touches; frills, as it were. One used that phrase to refer to more basic things, such as gates and stages. I told Joel I would come up the following morning.

Not five minutes after I hung up, my father called.

"When are you planning to go up to White Lake?" he asked.

"Tomorrow," I said, and then added, "Early," hoping that his question had been idle, knowing that it hadn't been, and flailing around for some way of changing his intention.

"Perfect," he said, like a knife in the ribs. "Billy and I will drive up with you."

I decided not to tell Joel. He enjoys surprises.

At 9:30 the following morning, my father and Billy arrived at 47 West 57th Street. Keith would have come, too, but he was attacking some new freeway project in San Francisco. Forewarned by a sympathetic secretary in my old man's office, I was downstairs to meet him or, more precisely, to head him off. He still hadn't visited the Woodstock offices, and he wasn't going to start today if I could help it. The time would pass slowly enough as it was. Of course, like all ordained pessimists, my father goes into a sort of hunting frenzy whenever he senses the nearness of evidence likely to confirm his worst suspicions, and he was by me and almost to the elevator before I could react. Fortunately, the limousine pulled up in front of the building just at that moment and, pleading an urgent need for haste, I managed to maneuver him into the car and away.

The ride up to Sullivan County passed in silence for the most part as the three of us took refuge in the contemplation of our abundant neuroses. I reflected on the fact that I was more nervous about my father's reaction to the site than I was about its actual condition, and I decided to have myself committed as soon as the Festival was over. Billy reflected on the possibility that he was about to see evidence of incompetence so overwhelming that his refusal to participate would be seen as culpable, and he considered having me committed before the Festival got started. My father busied himself trying to adopt an attitude of benign resignation toward the calamities he confidently expected to unfold, and tried to figure out a way of having everyone on the Woodstock staff committed before they could do further harm. It was a rollicking journey.

When we arrived in White Lake, I directed the chauffeur through the town to Hurd Road. I chose this approach to the site because it afforded a sudden and dramatic view of the performance area, assuming the performance area existed.

That was a good part of the problem. As we topped the rise, a stage some three weeks from completion came into view. Dozens of workmen scurried around, tapping and hammering without visible result. Then there were the fences, on which much time, money, and thought had been expended. They were up, all right. Complete. Gleaming. The only problem was that they were just a tad flimsy. Like, a herd of rampaging toddlers could have run right over them—and did, come to think of it. Then there was the audience. Yes, the audience. True, it was only Wednesday, but down there in the midst of our would-be performance area were some twenty thousand customers, camped. I suppose I should have been grateful that they weren't demanding entertainment, but I was too busy thinking of all the tickets I had brought up to sell.

Well, none of all this was lost on my father and Billy, and they said to me what everyone says to a man with a terminal illness: "Good luck. We'll be by the phone if you need us." Of course I did, and they were. For some reason, having discovered the worst, they relaxed into a pragmatic frame of mind and prepared to help.

John on Food for Love—II

On Tuesday, August 12, I received an excited, almost incoherent call from Jeff Joerger informing me that Woodstock was not living up to its agreement to build the food-concession stands to his specifications. He said there was a good chance that the stands would not be ready by the time the gates opened on Friday, and he alleged that Food for Love was not getting much in the way of co-operation from Peter Goodrich or anyone else on the Woodstock staff. He even muttered darkly about being "spied on" by Woodstock "goons," and said he had to see me up at the site as soon as possible.

The next day, as I have just related, I drove to White Lake with my father and brother. After recovering sufficiently from my shock at the general state of disarray in which I found everything, I took leave of my relatives and hurried off to the top of the rise behind the performance area, where the food stands were being constructed. Even from a distance they looked somewhat incomplete: crude ten-foot-square boxes with counters all around. Various suppliers' trucks stood nearby in the spot cleared for parking and delivery, but there was no food visible anywhere. A group of long-hairs was working feverishly in the vicinity: digging, hammering, etc., and off to one side I saw two of them who seemed to be having an argument. Four or five others were ranged around, watching with interest. I walked toward the angry little knot and recognized Joerger and Goodrich as the two combatants. Jeff's colleagues, Howard and Baxter, were watching them, as were two figures I can only describe as shady—even in the bright sunlight.

Jeff and Peter were yelling about the state of preparations, each accusing the other of reneging on various promises and understandings. I got the feeling that tempers were fraying fast, and Peter confirmed this impression by suddenly taking a swing and connecting with Joerger's mouth. As Jeff fell back, his two partners stepped forward, but a sudden languidly menacing movement by the two unknowns checked whatever violence they had in mind. Then Jeff spotted me, and he shot off the ground in my direction.

"You saw that," he shouted. "You saw him hit me. You think we're going to stand for that kind of shit? Like hell we are! We're pulling out. You guys can go fuck yourselves."

"Now wait a minute," I said. "It's obvious that things haven't been going well up here, but I'm sure that whatever problem you have, we can work it out."

Joerger sputtered and raged for a while and then said, "You're going to have to make some real concessions to us to make up for this kind of treatment we've been getting. If you want us to stay, there are going to have to be some changes in our contract, 'cause you guys have welshed on your part of the deal and we've had it up to here with you." He stormed off in the direction of his stands.

I turned to Goodrich. "I don't know what the hell is going on around here, but I want to get to the bottom of it fast. Where are Joel and Michael?"

He said they were at the Telephone Building waiting for me, and offered to drive me over. On the way to his car, he introduced his two aides as Lenny and Bob, giving me to understand that they were special security people Michael had hired to watch over all monies collected at the fair.

When I arrived in White Lake, Michael explained that the stands weren't ready because of the endless changes Food for Love kept demanding. Goodrich's people would do one thing and Joerger's people would say they should have done another, so they were finally told to hire workmen of their own. They had done just that, and now they were claiming that we should bear the cost.

Joel mentioned that a second and more serious problem revolved around Lenny and Bob, who were, it seemed, our experts in the prevention and detection of rip-offs. They had gone the day before to the food area to ask Joerger & Company such pertinent questions as: how was Food for Love planning to account for its sales; how was it going to guard its cash; where was it going to deposit its money; etc. Their inquiries had been greeted with suspicion and indignation. Countersuspicion, accusations, and hostility had been the result.

Michael was adamant that we should have a man at the food stands safeguarding our interests. I didn't disagree, but I thought it might be inflammatory, under the circumstances, for that man to be Lenny or Bob. Besides, there was a more pressing question on my mind.

"Who the hell *are* these people that we have to be so suspicious of them in the first place?"

Goodrich mumbled something about having made a mistake in judgment.

"But, Peter," I persisted, "you told me that you knew these people from way back. You told me they were experienced food handlers."

Nothing.

I figured I might as well know the worst. "Tell me honestly, Peter, what's the background on these guys?"

Goodrich winced angrily. "Joerger owns an antique shop in the Village, Baxter is a set designer, and Howard owns a small recording studio."

I stared at him.

"Now don't get the wrong idea, John. Both Jeff and Baxter have done food-concessionaire work in the past . . . in Miami."

Cronyism, hippie style, had come to the Age of Aquarius.

John on Last-Minute Frenzy—I

I very much wanted the Festival to be a big success, and on August 13, with one or two vital exceptions, already mentioned, most of the site was in readiness. The parking lots (rented pastures) were well marked and attended. The camping zones had been cleared. Areas had been designated for toilets, first aid, food delivery, and water tanks. In a large clearing in the woods, small concession stands had been built, providing a rustic hippie supermarket-retreat sort of thing—our Aquarian Shopping Esplanade. Paths in the forest had names like "Groovy Way" and "Aquarian Avenue," and just for tots a full five acres had been set aside as a playground. There were swings, Junglegyms, seesaws, sandboxes, and even a little mudhole: facilities that were used almost exclusively by adolescents during the concert, while the tots swam naked, smoked grass, and got into the music. Part of the five-acre-playground patch was converted into a zoolet and stocked with fetching little animals for the amusement of the flower children's children. We had lambs, piglets, chicks, a baby cow, etc. A rumor that the cow was eaten after the food stands were pillaged of their wares is still unconfirmed.

Preparations in the performance area, as I've suggested, were not so advanced. The concept had been for it to be surrounded entirely by a large impenetrable hurricane fence, solidly planted so no one could burrow under and high enough to frustrate all but the most determined vaulters. At intervals there were to have been openings, replete with turnstiles and ticket-takers and ticket-selling booths guarded by Pinkertons. We even had hand stampers, in case someone wanted to leave the performance area and return during the same show. Theoretically, the area was supposed to be cleared by our guards at the end of each day, and as an inducement to our patrons to leave, we had arranged for all entertainment to cease at these times, figuring that most people wouldn't find an empty stage all that transfixing.

This was all well and good, except for the fact that by Wednesday night some fifty thousand people had already arrived. The hurricane fences were up, to be sure, but the turnstiles and gates were not, so what we had was a nice long perimeter with a lot of nice big openings and nobody to say boo to anyone who felt like walking in. And a whole mess of people felt like it. Once inside, they could sit and watch several hundred frantic long-hairs swarming over the stage and applying some last-minute finishing touches such as lights and sound equipment and a roof. In addition, knowing that there was a lot more audience where they just came from, they wanted to get good seats—and that meant that they weren't intending to leave. To give them credit, since our food, water, and sanitary facilities were all well within the perimeter, there was no reason why they should.

We simply had not had enough time. Then, too, it had

rained almost nonstop since our arrival in White Lake, and that
had aggravated things. Michael, who had the primary responsibility, had established the stage and the performers' pavilion as his
highest priorities, and Joel and I had been so damned busy with
tickets, land acquisitions, town meetings, lawsuits, public relations, and just trying to get the thing to happen somehow that
we had not been able to stand there and personally make sure
the turnstiles got built and manned by Monday, the 11th. I
forget what Artie was busy doing.

As I've indicated, by the time I arrived on Wednesday, the
situation was well out of hand. I might have been able to salvage
something if I'd been able to concentrate on the gates exclusively, but such an indulgence was out of the question. I did
manage to get together a crew of about twenty bodies to plant
the turnstiles and place the ticket booths in their proper spots.
At the same time, I gathered up some of our security people,
filched from stage-guarding duties, and asked them to keep
watch on all the perimeter openings. I requested several others
to take bullhorns and pass through our hordes of early arrivals
with instructions to decamp. These men were invariably pounced
on and obliterated.

Meanwhile, outside, people without tickets were directed
to a temporary kiosk where some of the girls from the office
stood ready to sell. When the prospective purchasers got a look
at the crowd within, however, and at the multitude of poorly
guarded openings, they tended to sidle away into the darkness,
leaving muffled mutters of "Later, man" lingering in the air
behind them.

Undaunted, we worked on until one of the twenty or so
entrances was finally completed. As we were moving our equipment to the next opening, Michael drove up on his motorcycle
to say that we had an urgent land problem and my presence was
required immediately. Away, reluctantly, I went. When I got
back to my crew, it wasn't. The gates were wide open and
unguarded, and the crowd had grown. In addition, some of the
hurricane fencing had come down, creating our twenty-first
entrance. One of the Pinkertons who was standing around doing

nothing about anything offered his opinion that we just were not going to do much ticket-collecting that weekend. I complimented him on his acuity and went snarling off to collect more workers.

I had no sooner begun trudging down the road than Wes Pomeroy accosted me. He wanted to discuss the dire straits we were in as a result of the New York City police pulling out, which I'll go into later. I told him I was more concerned about gates and tickets. He looked at me kind of funny and said, "John, I think you should realize once and for all that you're not going to get those gates up and collect your money. I've been involved with a lot of crowds in my time. I can feel them: how they'll react, what they'll want. You try getting these people out of the performance area now and you'll have a riot on your hands. So let's just concentrate on what's feasible."

I remember feeling an eerie sensation of relief at that moment. The accomplishment of an impossible task had been declared impossible. So be it. We were going to end up in the red and that was that. Finis. "O.K., Wes. Let's go talk about security."

The Food for Love problem still had to be solved that evening as well. Around midnight, Joel and I got a hurry-up summons to meet Michael and Artie over at the concession stands. When we pulled up to the Food for Love encampment, our partners told us that Joerger & Company had in retrospect become even more incensed about the day's events. What I had hoped was only wild talk about packing up and leaving was threatening to become reality. For the moment, however, saner counsel was prevailing, and the food boys were working on an alternative for us. I had a hunch it wasn't going to do much for my appetite. I got out a walkie-talkie and called Wes Pomeroy right away. He said it sounded to him like we were going to have to bite whatever bullet they fired, and advised us to be agreeable but noncommittal about whatever they might suggest. Meanwhile, he said, he would get on the phone to the local FBI office and find out if they could arrange with the government to airlift food into White Lake if the worst happened. "Why the FBI?" I asked. "Who else?" said Wes. Stupid question, I guess.

I repeated Wes's instructions to Joel, Michael, and Artie, and we chatted idly while awaiting the pleasure of the F for L'ers, who were huddling conspiratorially inside their trailer. Below us stretched the performance area; now, like the moon, almost one quarter full. Small fires had been started by some in the audience in order to keep themselves warm against the surprisingly cool night. Other fires dotted the outlying camping areas perched on the surrounding hills. Occasionally, music would come floating up—smells, too: meat, grass, excrement from the nearby Johnnys-on-the-Spot. Considering the exertions of the day—and what was still to come—it was a beguilingly peaceful moment. The armies were at rest, the battle two days' distant.

My personal calm was shattered by the appearance of Weingrad, who beckoned us into the trailer where his clients were waiting. They had a take-it-or-leave-it offer for us, which they prefaced with a review of all the various transgressions of which Woodstock was guilty and which we prefaced with a proposal to compensate them for their extra expenses out of our share of the profits. Of course it was too late for compromises of that sort, and so we were forced at last to ask them what exactly it would take to soothe their lacerated sensibilities. "Everything" was the answer. They would return our $75,000 and keep all of the profits from the sale of food. We expressed outrage at this. They just smiled and gave us ten minutes to cut the crap and agree. Remembering Wes's advice, I told them that they had us over a barrel and that we would have to go along. However, we wanted the whole thing formalized and we weren't expecting our lawyer until Friday. They said that was O.K. by them because if, come Friday, we still hadn't signed, they could still walk out and we'd be in even more of a hole. (They were wrong about that; by Friday, nobody was going anywhere.) We said curt good nights and left.

It had been quite a day. In the space of twelve hours we had lost our two major sources of revenue. Who knew what we might accomplish in the space of the next four days?

John on Last-Minute Frenzy—II

For me the Festival began at precisely that moment when I first realized that nothing I could do could possibly make any difference. On August 13 I was still under the illusion that gates could be erected, tickets sold, attendance controlled, food dispersed, and an over-all profit made. By August 14 I knew better. I understood that we were engaged in a last-ditch holding operation. The Festival was most decidedly going to happen. Only the issue of our eventual survival of it was now in doubt.

I was staying in a shabby old motel on Route 17B and was awakened Thursday morning by the sound of honking horns. On stumbling outside I discovered that the inbound lane coming from the Quickway was almost bumper to bumper. Wes and I were supposed to visit the FBI office in Monticello that morning to discuss food supplies, and I decided that he and I had better get moving before traffic became tied up on the outbound lane, too. We warily watched the building up of cars on our left as we drove the ten or so miles into town. Yes, we admitted to each other, it looked like the weekend was going to be a little busier than expected.

On our arrival at the FBI office, we were greeted by two agents who were careful, polite, and, by their own estimate, powerless to help us. They suggested a gigantic milk and rice distribution to cope with any last-minute desertion by our concessionaires. The milk could be obtained from local farmers, most notably Max Yasgur. The rice . . . well, maybe the Army might help out. A better idea was that we go along with Food for the duration and then sue afterward. In the meantime, the Bureau would make up a shopping list just in case.

Taking leave of the G-men, Wes and I found a lightly traveled side road that brought us back to White Lake without too much delay. Once there, I went to the Telephone Building and called Paul Marshall's office in New York to explain the Food situation. Our attorney agreed that we were forced to go along and promised to join us the following morning. I advised him that he had better leave in the evening if he wanted to keep that promise. He said he would.

The next item on my agenda was security. The New York City policemen we had hired originally had been forbidden to come to the Festival. Nevertheless, word had gotten around that we were paying fifty bucks a day to anyone who defied the ban, and some of the less fastidious bulwarks of law and order jumped at the opportunity. It was an easy way to make $150, they reasoned, and nobody ever had to find out about it. They used aliases, presenting themselves at the Telephone Building as Michael R. Mouse, Irving Zorro, R. T. Tin, etc. No John Smiths showed up, because, as one of them confided to me, "Ya don't wanna be too cute."

When all the various television and comic-strip heroes had arrived, Wes, his assistant, John Fabbri, and I instructed them on their duties for the weekend. These duties included keeping the peace, helping people in distress, assisting the staff of doctors and nurses, clearing paths for ambulances, seeing that areas were cleared for helicopter take-offs and landings, and guarding the stage, the performers, and all the land we *hadn't* rented. They did not include busting people, whether for drug offenses, nudity, obscene gestures, or outright balling. People on bad drug trips were to be handled gently until someone with experience could be found to talk them down.

All security personnel were issued special red T shirts emblazoned with our dove-and-guitar emblem. I learned after the Festival that many of the New York City cops thus attired spent the entire weekend drinking and screwing. Many more worked hard and well. All had a very good time.

After security had been dealt with, I turned my attention to the various medical and legal-aid arrangements. We had hired Dr. Abruzzi to supervise our health services, and he in turn had hired several other young doctors and nurses. All in all, we had about thirty or forty medical people on hand, many of them with experience in handling outdoor events such as ours. While cuts, bruises, and the like were expected to account for the bulk of the work, we all felt that the most serious problems would be drug-related. We decided, accordingly, that the medics should team up with the expert members of the Hog Farm to talk people down off bad acid trips. The combination represented, we hoped, sufficient manpower to handle what we all felt certain was going to be a record number of bummers. And, in this area at least, we were right.

On the legal front, we had arranged for ten young lawyers from the New York Legal Aid Society to come up to White Lake and act as public defenders. We knew there would be a fair number of busts in and around the Festival, and we didn't want a lot of young people languishing in jail over the weekend just because they didn't have a lawyer or didn't know their rights or were simply too damned stoned to think of anything to say when they came before a judge. The lawyers were aided in their work by the decency of the local District Attorney, who recognized early on that many of our customers would be using illegal drugs, but who also recognized that such use would be among the least of his and our problems over the course of the weekend. He acted, therefore, with compassion and good grace throughout.

That night I went out to dinner with Wes and finally got a chance to ask him exactly what had happened to our security force. He told me that he had originally applied to an old friend of his high up in the New York City police hierarchy for permission to hire off-duty cops for the Festival. After some hedging and thumb-twiddling, the permission had been granted, and in mid-July Wes and John Fabbri had set up a series of interviews in New York. The word had been passed that we were offering good money, and so roughly two thousand cops showed up to fill some four hundred places. Wes had wanted to stress a hands-off helpful attitude rather than a militant law-enforcement posture, and his questions in the interviews were designed to weed out hard-core law-and-order types. Question: What do you do when a long-hair comes up to you and blows marijuana smoke in your face? Wrong answer: Bust the mothah in the teeth and haul his ass in. Right answer: Close your eyes, inhale, and smile. Et cetera. The interviewing lasted three days, and at the end of that time we had our peace-keeping force—we thought.

On Monday, August 11, our friend in the police hierarchy had a heart attack. The first thing that came to the attention of his temporary replacement was our plans for the weekend. The department had been getting a lot of flak about that time on the subject of moonlighting, and the replacement decided that the time was ripe to crack down. Thus, with much attendant fanfare, he issued his restraining order and our troops evaporated. Yet again, our best-laid plans had gang a-gley.

Wes and I finished dinner in somber silence and then returned to the Telephone Building to meet with the local Sheriff. He told us that traffic was becoming so snarled that he doubted whether anyone, performers included, would be able to reach the performance area by Friday afternoon—unless they walked, or flew. This bit of intelligence galvanized us into contacting several helicopter services. We soon had at least two choppers firmly reserved, and Wes got a friend of his at West Point to promise us a bird or two in case things got really hairy. What all this was going to cost, I didn't want to know.

Joel on Last Minutes

When I presented myself at the office in White Lake on Monday, August 11, I was immediately pressed into service in so many areas that my head spun. Virtually no segment of the planning was on schedule. Each crew chief was working on a round-the-clock rush. Deliveries were coming in at all hours of the day and night. Requests for new purchases and additional staff deluged me. By Tuesday, I had come to the conclusion that certain events in life were not amenable to human control.

I did have one minor success. A three-hour meeting with a county health official finally got us an approval of our water supply. I remember having a lengthy discussion about our methods of making sure that the drinking water would be free of coliform. I still don't know what coliform is.

Very quickly after my arrival, word got around that I was available. People with unsolvable problems queued up outside my office door. Could we get Governor Rockefeller to lend us the Department of Transportation for the weekend? Could we fly in a large body of fresh water within the next forty-eight hours? If the food concessionaires dropped out at the last minute, could we arrange a rice-lift? I soon realized that the people asking these questions weren't interested in answers; it was their way of passing the problem on to me. I began bouncing all questions back to the askers. I had my own problems. I was merciless. I started acting, in short, like Michael.

The worst conditions obtained at the stage and fencing operations. Fences and gates were one of those silly flights of fancy that we greedy promoters had tried in vain to make into a reality. We would have done better with a chalk line and the honor system. But as badly off as we were in the fence department, we were worse off in stage construction. I used to hang around watching the construction gangs improvising as they went along. One of the engineers would sit down to figure out how long it would take to erect the plastic canopy over the stage and emerge from his calculations with the suggestion that we substitute a tarpaulin. This would get the problem off his back for the length of time it took to find a tarp big enough to cover a stage that had quadrupled in size since the early phases of planning. One morning as I watched, a bulldozer backed into one of the stage supports, putting a stylish bend in a previously straight pipe. "Far out!" said the bulldozer operator. A gang moved in to replace the pipe. I left, visions of liability-insurance policies dancing in my head.

Wednesday morning I was due at an early meeting to close on a strategic piece of land that we were renting from one Walter Hoeft, of Middletown. It happened to be the four acres across the road from the stage, the very plot that we were building our performers' pavilion on. Silly of Michael not to have rented it before.

The pavilion, of course, was the only area where construction was on schedule, and the negotiations with Mr. Hoeft went smoothly. He mentioned a very high figure. I countered with a reasonable figure, possibly a bit on the low side. Mr. Hoeft reiterated his first figure and added the English phrase "or else" just after the zeros. I capitulated. We signed. Shortly thereafter I discovered that this same plot of land had been on the market for two years and that the purchase price was roughly one half what we were paying for a three-day rental.

Then, for sheer terror, there were always the meetings with the boys from Food for Love. These confabs were devoted to the subject of safeguarding the cash taken in at the food stands, and they were well attended. Woodstock was represented by all its heavy security guards and ex-carnival hustlers. Food for Love needed no experts in the booth with them. There was much ill-tempered talk of scrip, cup-and-bun counting, and Brink's trucks. There was also an occasional are-you-calling-me-a-crook-you-sleazy-sonofabitch. The Food boys thoughtfully resolved the points at issue on Wednesday night by extracting from us a contract provision whereby Woodstock ended up with no profit participation. Since we no longer had a stake in the food gross, we didn't have to worry about food-gross security. Why we hadn't thought of that ourselves, I'll never know.

In this age of the telephone, who thinks about communications? When you want to talk to somebody, you just pick up the phone. Unless you're preparing a rock festival in the middle of an enormous farm. Then you have to string telephone lines to everywhere at great expense. And then, when you get the lines strung, all you have to do is talk into a receiver and somebody on the other end will respond. "Michael?" Or whoever. "Nope. Haven't seen him for an hour." This sort of thing used to drive me crazy until we hit on two neat solutions to the wandering-boss communications problem. Then the solutions used to drive me crazy.

We were approached by a portly insouciant purveyor of "one-of-a-kind" electronic items. He offered us a mobile telephone. Michael's eyes lit up. He loved gadgets. There was one available for immediate purchase, and after midnight there would probably be another. For $2,500. Were we interested? In a last-ditch effort to stay in touch with Michael, we bought one. After a ten-minute familiarization, he put it in his Porsche and zoomed off toward the latest crisis. Moments later, our extravagance was apparently rewarded when one of our suppliers called with an urgent question that only Michael could answer. "No sweat," I said. "Just hold on. I'll raise my partner on our new radio network."

One thing about these newfangled contraptions: you have to turn the power switch to "on." Michael never did. Twenty-five hundred dollars versus the human element, and the human element won. The mobile phone disappeared before the Festival began.

Walkie-talkies were something else again. They were purchased in great numbers and disappeared as rapidly as they were purchased, until we began deducting $130 apiece from staff salary checks for such absent-mindedness. When they were working, these walkie-talkies came in very handy. When they weren't working—and even in the days before Friday they broke down regularly—they were sent to the Reverend Ganoung, who, among his other talents, had mastered the art of walkie-talkie repairing. The things ran for about eight minutes of conversation before draining the juice from the ten pen-light batteries that powered them. For those eight minutes, however, they were dynamite. I was assigned the code name "Woodstock One." "Woodstock Command, this is Woodstock One. Over . . ." It had a nice ring to it.

Thursday morning bright and early I was on my way out of the office for another depressing inspection tour when a snatch of conversation between Michael and John Morris, our stage manager, caught my ear. They were chatting about the size of the herd slouching toward Bethel. To the best of my knowledge we had sold sixty-six thousand three-day tickets as of August 8. Working with a standard two-to-one advance sale ratio, I had estimated that there would be roughly one hundred thousand guests at our garden party. Michael and Morris thought otherwise.

"Have you been out to the site yet this morning, fellah?" Morris asked Michael.

"No. Why?" Michael responded.

"Oh, nothing. Except there are about fifty thousand people already camped in front of the stage."

Michael giggled. "It's gonna be a monster."

I felt a sudden urge to make a phone call or twenty. Something inside me had snapped: my confidence. One by one I dialed the numbers of friends and relatives to whom I'd sent complimentary tickets, and one by one I dissuaded them from coming to the Festival.

At least kith and kin would be safe. Fifty thousand people! The Festival wasn't even due to start for another thirty-six hours.

Over at the site, Jock was having a fanciful conversation with one of the heads of security about how to move the advance crowd out of the performance area so that we could make them buy tickets after the fences were erected. It makes me laugh to think about it.

The fairgrounds seemed to be swarming with photographers. They couldn't all have been hired by Michael. Some of them appeared to be bona fide press. I marveled at the intuition that had gotten them up to the site early. Those "before" photos were going to look great in court.

Unaccountably, the area we had set aside for a field hospital and first-aid center was in a state of near readiness. Dr. Abruzzi had been ruthless in his demands for construction gangs and materials. That Thursday he showed no signs of slowing down. He collared me as soon as I got out of my car.

"Did you see those kids in the performance area? There must be thousands of them."

"Fifty thousands at last count."

"Jesus! This is going to be a big one."

"Are you ready to go, Bill?"

"I thought so until this morning, but it looks like we might have twice the crowd we expected. Twice! Hell, there's no way to tell how big it's going to be. We're gonna need more staff and more supplies, and fast. To begin with, we've got to have . . ."

"Anything you want, Bill. Just let me know when you order so I can make sure the check is ready."

"Terrific! We'll take care of our end."

Music to my ears.

I got back to my car and headed toward Hurd Road. Down by the woods that separated the performance area from the campgrounds were a number of busy long-hairs constructing the dry-goods concession booths. Power lines were being strung and hammering was proceeding at a brisk staccato. Something about the activity suggested more a battening down of hatches than a preparation for business. I drove on.

Back at the office the usual throng had gathered with questions and insults. The faces were getting familiar. There was Harold Pantel with an urgent query about the electrical-contract payment. Over near the door to my office, a truck driver with a delivery receipt for thousands of feet of plastic pipe was waiting for my signature. Lee Mackler, secretary to the Woodstock power elite, trundled toward me pushing a wheelbarrow full of fresh phone messages.

A pleasant roundish chap from a Boston firm called Intermedia Systems, Inc. cornered me to talk about a plan for busing people into the performance area from the outer parking lots. The scheme was designed to keep as many cars out of the central area as possible. I liked it until I heard the price: $18,000, provided we could rent enough buses on a summer weekend. "Forget it," I said. "We don't have that kind of money for buses. They'll have to walk." "Who's gonna walk eight miles to get to your Festival?" he asked.

Somehow Len Kaufman and I ended up having dinner together at a roadside restaurant far enough from the site so that I could relax a few notches. Lenny was the kingpin of our "heavy" security cadre, a segment of the Woodstock task force that we tried to keep under wraps. This group was made up of ten beefy fellows skilled in the martial arts. Many of them carried little paper bags around in which were concealed "pieces," *i.e.*, their snub-nosed revolvers. All of them had callouses on the edges of their hands and plenty of tattoos. Their former callings included armored-truck guard, bouncer in a rough nightclub, foreman in a prison machine shop, and respected leader of a well-known motorcycle gang. Lenny, their boss, was very personable. We actually had a nice time at dinner. He displayed a condescending skepticism toward our plans for a nonviolent security force, the one Wes Pomeroy had assembled, but he made it clear that he was hoping for a hassle-free three days. Of course, if any of the fairgoers were in the mood for "jive," Lenny's cats would be ready to accommodate them. I shuddered at the image.

Heading back toward the site, me behind the wheel, Lenny and his paper bag on the seat to my right, I felt like I was driving back to a city under siege. We arrived just after dark and Jock was waiting for me outside the Telephone Building. He had a big grin on his face, and it occurred to me that it was the first smile I'd seen in days. What an odd thing to do with one's mouth.

"Nero fiddled; you grin like an idiot," I greeted him.

"I've got something that's going to lift your spirits, O Most Rosenman," he proclaimed, and led me around the side of the building to where two brand-new motorcycles were parked.

"Whose are these?" I asked.

"Ours."

"Ours?"

"Yup. This is our transportation for the next three days. I think they're going to come in very handy."

"You know what I think?"

"You think we should take them out for a little test drive just to make sure they're in working order."

"Precisely. Let's go check out our vast parking acreage."

"O.K. But there's just one little problem: no helmets."

"How come?"

"I don't know. Nobody thought to get helmets. Do you think we need them?"

Of course we needed helmets. And gates, and more staff, and another half-million dollars, and two more weeks for construction . . .

"To hell with helmets," I said.

"I second the motion," Jock replied. "And I hope the judge agrees."

We set out on a grand tour of the parking lots, ten huge fields that had been rented during the previous two weeks. As the moon rose, the temperature dropped into the bracing zone. We stopped to chat with an attendant, a kid from Minnesota who had hitchhiked east to work at the Festival. He had a lonely job, and he was grateful for any conversation. In his mind there was no question that we were on the eve of something big. Everybody in Minnesota had been talking about Woodstock for months, he told us. I noticed that he was shivering. All he had on was a T shirt and jeans. I asked him if he wanted some blankets or a jacket. He was embarrassed to say yes, but common sense got the better of him. I got the office on my walkie-talkie and told them to send some blankets and sandwiches out to Lot 4. Who says? they wanted to know. Woodstock One says, I answered with a tiny surge of pleasure.

Jock and I got rolling again, over the miles of empty back roads that separated one dairy farm from another. Toward midnight we reached the top of a hill and stopped. We killed the motors on our bikes and looked around. The silence spread out from us in waves. Neither of us said a word.

PROGRESS (?) REPORT: AUGUST 15

LAND: Max Yasgur's farm and various adjoining bits and pieces; 600 acres total

STAFF: Same as July give or take 300 additional construction workers, 350 off-duty New York City policemen incognito, and several hundred early arrivals at the Festival

TICKET RECEIPTS: $1,107,936

TALENT BOOKINGS: All present and accounted for except Iron Butterfly

ATTORNEYS: Same as July—but busier

PORTABLE TOILETS: 2,000—very popular

MONEY SPENT: $2,135,761

A QUARIUS!

"... and lo, a great multitude, which no man could number ..."
—*Revelation* VII:9

In the past, similarly innumerable miltitudes had congregated together only for the purpose of accomplishing a well-defined objective—at Marathon and Gaugamela, for example, at Cannae and Pharsalus, Agincourt and Waterloo. Now, however, concentrated on a few square miles of farmland and more populous than Omaha or Oakland or Oklahoma City, there was this sudden agglomeration that was just sitting there, content to all appearances, simply to constitute itself and Be. "What kind of a culture is it," the *New York Times* was moved to ask, "that can produce so colossal a mess?"

On Thursday afternoon, there were so many straws in the wind that they looked like haystacks. "I've never seen anything like this," said a bus-company official in New York City, "... never so many thousands going to one place."

Up at the one place, close to a hundred of the so many thousands had already arrived, and the best estimates were that several hundred more thousands were on their way. Route 17B was stationary as far back as the Quickway, and the Quickway itself would soon be backing up as well, mile after inexorable mile. "TRAFFIC UPTIGHT AT HIPPIEFEST" was how the *Daily News* described the situation, and the *News*, as always, was Right On.

Traffic wasn't the only thing that was uptight, however; there was also Wesley ("Lesley," according to "New York's

Picture Newspaper") Pomeroy. Wes was uptight because some three hundred and fifty off-duty New York City policemen he'd recruited to maintain law and order at the hippie fest had been ordered off the job by their commissioner. "Now I don't have any security people at all," he wailed. "We're having the biggest collection of kids there's ever been in this country, without any police protection."

It was no laughing matter. The Hell's Angels and numerous other like-minded cherubim had arrived. So had Abbie Hoffman and a contingent of Yippies. "No Trespassing" signs were being ignored wholesale, and local farmers were, literally, up in arms. Food and water were clearly going to be in short supply, sanitary facilities overtaxed, tempers short, drugs overabundant. Worst of all, there was no way for anyone who wanted to, to leave. The whole state of affairs, in short, was pungently nitroglyceral; "hopeless," as one state trooper put it, "and getting worse."

And the music hadn't even started yet.

But already there were countersigns. The ads had promised three days of Peace and Music to a generation whose political and social awareness dated from the assassination of John F. Kennedy, whose adolescence had been coterminous with hellishly bitter warfare in Vietnam and America's ghettos, whose few heroes—Malcolm X, Martin Luther King, Robert Kennedy, Eugene McCarthy—had been cut down one after another by bullets or "the system," whose efforts to change the system had, apparently, failed to the point of fostering reaction, and whose refuge from a world gone mindlessly malevolent lay in drugs, naïve mysticism, primal rhythm . . . and each other. In the summer of 1969 it was a generation that was unconsciously yet eagerly awaiting an opportunity to test itself, to put the values it had derived from the experience of the sixties into practice, to demonstrate to a hostilely skeptical adult constituency that it was real, that it was viable, and, above all, that it was *better* than what had gone before. It was a generation that was ready to move the world. All it lacked—up to the fifteenth of August— was a place to stand.

"Shopkeepers, local workmen, contractors, people on the street say they have been 'amazed at the politeness of the kids,' " the Washington *Post* reported on that day. "The kids say they're amazed that they're amazed."

Michael Lang declared, "The Festival is being done by the people who are the culture," and his assistant added, "If it comes out the way we dreamed it, then people are going to have a different view of this culture, of us."

A Hog Farmer summed it up: "Violence would be stupid. That's all 'they' need to put us down."

As the time for the music approached, an unidentified youth started climbing toward the top of a lighting tower. He kept on despite warnings from the stage, and the crowd cheered his progress. With each new rung, the tower swayed more and more, until, at the top, the young man was virtually freewheeling through the air. Then, suddenly, in the grip of some *folie de joie*, he let go, and hung for a moment suspended in the sky. Then he plunged eighty feet to the ground—and survived.

Not long afterward, Richie Havens stepped onto the stage. To him had fallen the honor of keynoting the Festival, and he echoed the boy on the tower and the surging sense of expectation that was sweeping through the audience.

"FREEDOM! . . ." he exulted. "FREEDOM! . . . FREEDOM! . . . FREEDOM! . . ." he bellowed into the microphone. And the sound system piled wattage onto his voice and blew it out into the ears of the generation on the hillside, the unprecedented hundreds of thousands who at that instant grasped the wonder of their emancipation. They had arrived. They were legion. They had burst free of the confines of their civilization and were finally, miraculously, their own. The test they had unknowingly been waiting for was now. Nothing could control them—except themselves. Nothing could defeat them—except their failure. There, at that moment, they assumed their covenant: come rain, come hunger, come thirst, come fatigue; come anything that might out of the hand of Nature—they would prove that the children of Aquarius were a nation.

And rain did come, and cold, and hunger, and the rest. As

Friday gave way to Saturday, the hillside and the land around it turned into mud. The field of Armageddon became a quagmire. Tens of thousands more people had arrived. Tens of thousands were still coming—despite the traffic, despite a radio appeal for them to stay away, despite everything. The medical staff, deluged by the first of what would eventually amount to more than five thousand health problems, sent out a desperate call for reinforcements. There were lines thirty minutes long for a drink of water, an hour long for a toilet, two hours long for a pay phone. As crisis after crisis arose and was reported down the wires to New York and the nation, one conclusion seemed unavoidable: disaster was on the way.

It must have gotten stuck in traffic. It didn't arrive on Saturday, at any rate. On the contrary, Saturday witnessed a dawning of the realization that the Festival was making it. The music started at twenty minutes past one in the afternoon and went on until half past nine Sunday morning. The performers, inspired by the size and responsiveness of their audience, gyrated around the stage like creatures possessed.

Toward sunset, Max Yasgur, the founder of the feast, came forward to deliver the benediction.

"I'm a farmer," he began, and the generation roared its approval. "I don't know how to speak to twenty people at one time, let alone a crowd like this . . . but I think that you people have proven something to the world. . . ." The hillside stirred; suddenly expectant. "That half a million kids can get together and have three days of fun and music . . ." The expectancy massed into sound. "And have *nothing but* fun and music. And I God Bless You for it!"

There was a bursting, an eruption, a jubilant typhoon of decibels, which rolled down on the balding farmer and reverberated from the hills beyond. They had come through. Somehow, so soon, it was official. And the truth of their vindication was manifest: it was not the result of their conscious efforts to be more, figuratively, than they really were; it was the proof, rather, of their constant, though inchoate, refusal to be less. What the hell else besides fun and music were half a million of them supposed to have on a pastoral summer weekend, after all? I mean, what sort of people did the world think they were? Adults?

Now there was only celebration. They had gloried in the challenge; they would revel in the triumph.

The most exalted of their grand heresiarchs led them: Janis Joplin, Creedence Clearwater Revival, the Grateful Dead, the Who. It was Saturday-Night America; the right people in the right place at the right time.

"This is the largest crowd of people ever assembled for a concert in the history of the world," said John Morris from the stage as 3:00 A.M. approached. "But it's so dark out there we can't see you and you can't see each other. So when I say 'three' I want every one of you to light a match. O.K.? Everybody got your matches? One . . . two . . . THREE!"

And there was an elevation of the host, a crescent transubstantiation of darkness into light, a glow neither celestial nor infernal, but human, achingly beautifully human, human almost to the point of tears.

The moment passed, but as the glow dissipated into the night air, the kliegs illuminated the figure of Sylvester "Sly" Stone. In this rightest of all places and times, here was the rightest man. Whether by accident, design, or instinct, his hand moved unerringly to the crowd's celebratory nerve. He wanted to take them where they wanted to go: Higher!

Prancing, dancing, coaxing, cajoling; an ecstatic daemon bathed sensual by the purple-filtered floodlights, Sly worked on his audience like a consummate hetaera on a young man's body. He offered pleasure. He demanded Dionysian abandon in return—and got it. Bright flashes of exhilaration illuminated the hillside like fireworks: hands, faces, eyes, bodies leapt into incandescence and were swept up into a bonfire of sound and feeling.

"I wanna take you higher . . ." Sly chanted, and the crowd answered him, "HIGHER!!!" again and again, each time from a more rarefied eminence, until height and depth lost meaning and there was only the moment, the eternally transient Now of existence suffusing the mingled thousands with a sense of fruition, of communion, and of reward.

That was the climax. The music went on until daylight, then resumed Sunday afternoon. But the tribes were disbanding. They had gotten what they'd come for; there was no more to be had. True, one could stay to savor the achievement or re-evoke the mystery's shadow, but the rain came down in torrents, and all around one could see that the generation was dwindling.

It ended Monday morning with Jimi Hendrix playing before the remnants of the weekend, animate and (mostly) otherwise. As he played, the audience he had missed was fanning out across the continent. Mournfully, Hendrix concluded his performance with a rendition of "The Star-Spangled Banner." The children of Aquarius, having proven something to the world, were now, with reluctance, on their way back to America.

THREE DAYS OF PEACE AND MUSIC

John on the Festival—I

Friday morning I looked out my motel window and beheld an eerie sight. Route 17B, pavement and shoulders, was packed with stationary cars, some of them abandoned, others serving as miniature Holiday Inns. It was 8:00 A.M., but along this entire stretch of massed motionless metal there was not a sound. A few people were up, just sitting quietly in their automobiles or building little fires along the side of the road to make coffee.

I got on my motorcycle and threaded my way into White Lake. There everything was humming. The main order of business was to see to it that all of this first day's acts were accounted for. As I arrived, the head of the stage-construction crew announced that with luck we would be ready to start rolling around four o'clock in the afternoon. Joel, John Morris, and I huddled and made our first tentative decision about keeping the music going nonstop. As we talked and planned, I began to think of the huge crowd some three miles' distant. Four hundred thousand people, it was estimated: some kind of powerful alien beast. To placate it and keep it docile became the philosophy of the weekend.

Back on my Honda, I wended my way toward the site. It took me thirty minutes to arrive at Food for Love's compound overlooking the cauldron. Below me there was a virtual carpet of humanity flowing up and down and across the performance area. I could see red-shirted Woodstock employees scurrying around on the stage. It looked like we might just be ready on time.

It didn't take me long to sign the articles of capitulation in Food's trailer, and I certainly didn't want to spend any more time there than I had to. I thought it a marvelous coincidence, therefore, that at the moment I stepped back into the sunlight, the mikes on the stage started working and John Morris's voice split the skies. "Ladies and Gentlemen, the promoters of this concert, Woodstock Ventures, have declared this a free festival. A free festival. The show's on us. We'll be getting it on at four this afternoon, so please be patient with us till then." There was no irony in his voice, but there was something very like it in the raucous cheer that went up from the crowd. It certainly was neat the way the official recognition of our food-concession and ticket-sales debacles came off in such close succession.

I got on my bike and headed down to the stage area. Whereas forty-eight hours ago there had been only confusion, now there was the additional factor of panic. The stagehands were frantically wiring and testing. Lights were being strung up and taken down and strung up again. People were stumbling over a large tarpaulin that was being readied for service in case of rain. They were tripping on it, bumping it into other structures on the stage, knocking each other over with one end of it when they tried to move the other—it was like a Keystone Cops comedy.

Off to one side of the stage was the performers' pavilion, a tepeelike structure designed to house and comfort our acts and the press. It was closely guarded and I had a bit of a hassle getting in, having misplaced my promoter's badge somewhere along with the key to my father's apartment. Luckily someone recognized me, and I was spared a memorable indignity and passed through the lines. Inside, there were tables and chairs and some portable stoves on which a private concessionaire was cooking up goodies for the cult figures and their entourages. All was calm, clean, and running smoothly there in contrast to the noise and dirt and chaos outside. Versailles early in 1789 probably seemed much the same.

On my way out of the pavilion, Michael hailed me. He was jovial to the point of unction, far-outing about this and that and radiating a supreme unconcern about everything. He was in his element. It was his scene. Those were his people listening to his music—even if it hadn't started yet. I saw later that he was quoted in the *Times* as saying something like "The people have come out of the streets and shown how beautiful it can be when we all get together for a groovy trip." I wondered whether this was all he had ever really wanted, and I asked him as much.

"No, man. Losing money is a bummer. But you can't tell how we're going to come out. This is a whole new thing. It's going to be the biggest thing that ever happened, and if we handle it right after it's over, we could make a pile."

"I think I've heard something like this before," I said.

He shrugged as if to say "Think what you like; I'm gonna groove," and walked away. "Oh, by the way," he said, turning in his tracks, "the guy with the rain insurance policy is over at my trailer. He needs your signature."

I brightened a little. I had forgotten about the rain insurance. We had had a devil of a time getting ourselves a policy, but our agent had finally been successful. Now, with all the precipitation threatening, it looked like we might have a winner.

"I'll go right over," I said.

"Groovy," Michael replied, and sauntered off. I didn't see him again until Tuesday.

The insurance man was waiting. I wrote out a check and he took it with a cheerful grin. "I think this is money well spent. The forecast for the weekend is cloudy skies with an eighty-per-cent chance of showers. You should make your money back and then some."

Very funny.

What I didn't fully comprehend was that in order to collect on rain insurance, one has to have a certain quantity of rain fall within the precise periods of coverage. Thus if one is covered from nine to five on a given Friday and it pours between eight and nine and five and six but only drizzles rheumily in between, you're screwed. More correctly, we're screwed. In keeping with the tone of the weekend, some Higher Being saw to that. The rain peaked during our time and valleyed during the insurer's. Thank you, Higher Being.

I left the insurance man fondling my money and headed off to see how our landlord was doing. I found Max in his house and in surprisingly good spirits. He was overflowing with praise for the kids. Both he and his lovely wife, Mims, seemed genuinely thrilled to discover that long-hair rock-freak kids were, by and large, polite and considerate humans. They expressed disgust for those of their neighbors who had barricaded themselves in their homes and broken out the ammunition. They didn't even seem to be worried about what was happening to their own property. "I've been adequately compensated," said Max. "If things don't quite add up after the weekend, we can all very easily sit down and do the right thing." Max was concerned, however, about all the drugs and about the possibility that we might not have a sufficient medical force. I told him about our preparations, and that seemed to quiet his fears for the most part. In any event, he wanted at some point to go down to the stage and welcome the gyrating hordes to his farm personally. Later on in the weekend, he did, as we said.

I spent two highly therapeutic hours with the Yasgurs and then headed back to headquarters. As things turned out, the show didn't actually get under way until around six. Richie Havens led off, and Joel and Wes and John Fabbri and I manned the phones down in White Lake trying desperately to co-ordinate the movements of the groups that were supposed to follow him. The problem was to make sure that everyone was assembled at his or her hotel or motel at the proper time to be helicoptered to the site. Once up there, it was Michael's and particularly Artie's responsibility to see to it that they were properly shepherded and coddled. After their performances, they were generally rounded up and flown right back to their lodgings.

All these movements involved a lot of good timing and co-ordination. There was only a limited supply of helicopters for the tasks at hand, and there were always emergency medical evacuations to contend with as well. On top of all that, calls for special supplies for performers and stagehands (some of them disgustingly trivial) and requests for transportation from the press, from members of our security forces, and from various and assorted groupies were constantly coming in. It kept us hopping, I can tell you. That first night, the night of August 15–16, we moved, in addition to Richie Havens, Joan Baez, Arlo Guthrie, Tim Hardin, the Incredible String Band, Ravi Shankar, Bert Sommer, and Sweetwater. Moreover, we had to spend an enormous amount of time placating angry hoteliers in connection with unruly long-hairs, dope (we couldn't have any of our performers busted, for God's sake), helicopter noise, and Lord knows what else. So hectic was the pace that it was only by accident that I happened to glance at my watch and discover that Friday had ended and there were only two more days to endure.

Joel on the Festival—I

The events of Thursday should have prepared me for Friday, but they didn't. I awoke around six to the sound of a herd of grazing automobiles being attacked by a swarm of motorcycles. A well-defined sense of foreboding washed over me. But the blue jeans I had been wearing all week nickered happily as I drew them on.

The Pines, the motel that a good part of the Festival staff inhabited during the first part of August, was located on Route 17B halfway between White Lake and Max's farm. It was about a hundred and fifty feet from the motel proper to the road, and a sizable portion of Detroit's annual output was visible from my doorstep. I felt the need of support and retreated back into the cabin to try to rouse Jock. He said semicoherently that he would join me later in White Lake and then resumed his troubled slumbers.

A moment later I was on my Honda, but going anywhere on 17B was more a matter of cartographic theory than geographic practice. What was normally a two-lane road that morning had three lanes of traffic heading in one direction—*facing* in one direction, I should say. I threaded my way cautiously against the grain, coming from time to time upon cars that had attempted to change lanes in some bygone era and become frozen in a diagonal heading. Once or twice I had to stop completely and walk my bike until I could find daylight to ride. There were other motorcycles on the road maneuvering through the lanes of cars. They were proceeding as slowly as I was, but in the opposite direction. Whenever we passed each other we smiled that secret smile that all motorcyclists display in traffic jams. The noise level was beginning to drop. People were just plain giving up on the concept of forward progress. Many were abandoning their cars and striking off for the Festival grounds on foot. Others were turning off their engines and going to sleep on their front seats. Horns stopped honking and arguments died away.

It took me about twenty minutes to cover the three or four miles from the motel to the office, and by the time I staggered into the Telephone Building I was ready to go back to bed. From the look of things, so was most of the rest of the staff. Sleeping bags and blankets littered the floor, many of them still harboring Woodstock employees. At a desk in the back room —our high-echelon inner sanctum—Lee Mackler and Don Ganoung were engaged in heated debate over some moot issue of community relations. Wes Pomeroy was already at his desk, and John Fabbri was just sitting down at his, his face so composed that it might have been just another day at the office for him. On my entrance everyone simultaneously stopped talking and inhaled. I remember having just enough time to think "Here it comes!" before it came. Ganoung had problems with the parking lots, the walkie-talkies, the landowners, and our corps of messengers. Mackler had problems with the payroll, the medical services, the water, the electricity, and an avalanche of phone calls from increasingly frantic parents. Pomeroy had problems dispatching security personnel, coping with gate crashers, coordinating action with the local police, and transporting talent from motels to the site. Wes's assistant Joe Fink, *in absentia*, had problems with a mild angina attack he had suffered earlier that morning, a development that added to Wes's anxieties, both personal and administrative. Helicopters were going to be needed, somebody declared. Where were we going to get them from and who the hell was going to pay?

I didn't really listen or respond to any of the questions. I just let them swirl over me, getting a feeling for the pace of the action. It was furious. Taking advantage of a pause in the torrent, I reached for the phone. "I'm dialing Santa Claus," I said. "Any of you people want anything special for Christmas?" There was a moment of shocked silence, then a relieved chuckle from one brave soul, and general laughter. We got down to work.

I improvised a rough system of priorities, putting all life-support systems first. Water problems were dealt with immediately, electrical snafus next. Wes and I worked out an assignment schedule for the security forces and were about to get into the business of helicopters when Jock arrived. Looking at his face, I got the impression that his trip to the office had resembled mine. After a few minutes of tripartite discussion, we decided to get as many helicopters as we could. Then we sat down with John Morris and worked out a revised performance schedule based on giving our customers as little free time as possible. We'll never know if that was really necessary. It's conceivable the kids would have maintained order, if not law, no matter what went on on stage.

After a bit more trouble-shooting on the tip of the iceberg, Jock grabbed his Honda keys and exited with a checklist of impossible missions to accomplish. I had taken root at my desk, a phone sprouting from each ear. Among the calls that were rolling in were some from the friends and relatives I had warned away the day before. A few of them wanted to thank me. The more adventuresome were a little miffed that I had dissuaded them from becoming eyewitnesses to history.

From time to time I would take a break and wander out to the front office. Most of the staff out there were sitting at rows of telephone-covered desks while a constant flow of humanity streamed through the front door. Kids looking for work, directions, handouts, posters, blankets, and what-have-you lined up at the reception desk. Most of them were sent away with a polite dismissal, but an occasional lucky one was pressed into service.

About midday telephone complaints began to come in in earnest from the local landowners. It seemed that a large number of unidentified people were trespassing, and what was Woodstock going to do about it? "Why, take care of it, of course," I invariably responded, patiently pretending to copy down name, address, and specific complaint. Although I realized that the farmers wouldn't wait too long before taking the law into their own hands, there was really nothing I could do except stall them.

Some time that afternoon, Richie Havens walked to the front of our mostly completed stage and threw out the first note of the concert. This event passed unnoticed at the office. Don Ganoung had fallen asleep over three disassembled walkie-talkies. Wes Pomeroy was busy pleading with a friend of his at West Point to lend us a chopper or two. And I was talking to Costa the courier about the crowd. Costa, being the owner of a motorcycle, was an important staff member during those desperate hours. He would shuttle back and forth between the site and White Lake seated majestically astride his Harley-Davidson. On the errand from which he had just returned he had picked up what I have since come to think of as a Woodstock Parable: The Evacuation of Our First Medical Emergency. A young girl hippie, having just been informed by her mother via long-distance telephone that if she didn't get out of that chaos *right now*, Daddy wasn't going to spring for her annual summer in Europe, insinuated herself between a truck and the fence toward which it was very gingerly backing. As soon as the rear bumper touched the denim fabric surrounding her plump young thigh, she let out a scream that wilted all mustaches within a thirty-yard radius. The truck driver, a shy family man from one of the neighboring towns, stopped his vehicle instantly and ran around to the back, where his worst fears were immediately exceeded. There on the ground almost beneath his wheels lay the motionless body of a young girl—she could have been his own daughter. From the still body came a moan. Medical help rushed to the scene. A doctor took charge. Every time they tried to move the girl, she screamed as though she were being raped by a porcupine. That settled matters as far as the doctor was concerned. He ordered an emergency evacuation by helicopter, the first one of the Festival. With the Wadleigh-Meurice cameras whirring, the poor broken body was strapped rigid to a board and lofted away toward Monticello and intensive care. When the chopper touched down, the victim was hastily unstrapped. At this point, flashing a brilliant smile and a cheerful thank-you, she sprang to her feet and ambled off toward the bus depot and Saint-Tropez.

Every now and then we would get a report on the progress of a certain blue truck that bore the name of the Tose Transportation Company, of Fairview, New Jersey. This vehicle was carrying tens of thousands of copies of our elaborately produced program booklet, which we had hoped to distribute to our patrons as souvenirs. The booklet described the acts that would be appearing and included a list of credits for the production. If I had had trouble covering four miles on a Honda, imagine the difficulties that the driver of this tractor-trailer was experiencing. Every couple of hours he would phone in. "I'm on the Quickway," he would say, or "I've reached the Monticello exit." It became a sort of sick joke in the office. Whenever things got really heavy, someone was certain to pop up with: "Where do you think the Tose truck is now?" Soon the helicopter pilots picked up on this gallows humor. The truck moved so slowly—and so seldom—that it became something like a feature of the terrain or a checkpoint: "I'm heading west over 17B. Will start my pattern at the Tose truck." Before long, an informal pool materialized, the idea being to peg the time of the truck's arrival at the site. There were no takers for Friday or Saturday and only a few for Sunday afternoon. Late Sunday and early Monday got most of the action.

By evening, the Reverend Don Ganoung's faith had begun to crumble. He had worked so hard on readying the parking lots, and now they were being misused. Reports came in that some were filled with campers and others with nothing at all. Even the arrival of hero sandwiches around dinnertime failed to lift his spirits. Wes, meanwhile, was too busy to be dejected. He had had Renee prepare a satchelful of cashier's checks for the NYC cops who had shown up to work at the Festival despite the no-moonlighting order promulgated earlier that week. Somebody trustworthy had to take them out to the site, since they were made out in blank, and I leaped at the opportunity to get a look at the crowd.

Moments later, the satchel strapped to my back, I was zigzagging my way along the shoulder of 17B toward whatever it was we had wrought. I feared the columns of bedraggled pedestrians. I would have been furious had I been in their shoes, and since they *were* in their shoes, I was glad to be traveling incognito. Every so often I had to use my horn, but I confined myself to the lightest and least insolent of taps. Still, somewhere in my head it must have registered that none of the people I saw on this journey seemed very threatening.

As I turned onto Hurd Road, I passed a roadblock manned by two of our "heavy" security guys. They were having no difficulty persuading cars not to turn in. Even motorcycle gangs waned obedient after a few weak attempts to intimidate Lenny's lieutenants. One of these two examined my Executive Pass suspiciously, but finally permitted me inside.

Here the going was even slower. There were no stationary vehicles, just enormous tides of people shifting and ebbing in response to unseen forces. The general direction of humanity seemed to be toward the stage, and that was close enough to where I wanted to go so that I was able to drift along with it. Forward progress at speeds in excess of the mob was impossible. For the next half hour, during which I covered roughly a quarter of a mile, I had to keep both feet on the ground and sort of waddle my way along with the Honda merely idling. It was getting dark, and the lights that we had strung up around the grounds were on, giving an eerie cast to the already bizarre appearance of the revelers. Leather and rags and denim made up the predominant motif, along with one-feather Indian headdresses, war paint, fringed chaps, moccasins, etc. The whole scene brought to mind visions of Washington Square being overrun by Comanches on a summer Sunday; peacefully overrun, that is. There were no scuffles and no discouraging words. And the skies were not . . . well, almost.

I finally reached the food stands at the top of the hill overlooking the performance area. They were blindingly lighted hives of activity. Hot dogs and hamburgers went from one side of the counters to the other with choreographed speed. In my stomach, my hour-old hero sandwich did a little fandango. The idea of eating a frankfurter prepared by Food for Love gave me shooting pains in my Boy Scouts' oath.

As I marveled at how tightly packed the humanity in the area of the food stands seemed to be, I looked down the hill toward the stage. It was my first glimpse of our natural amphitheater since the day before. Stretching the entire distance from the stands to the stage and out to the sides as far as I could see were four hundred thousand people. They looked like a thick carpet of gently seething paramecia; an ocean of grayish protoplasm momentarily placid, but capable of anything. Then the music came on: a blast of pure rock, and the ocean responded with a roar that was both effortless and monumental. A strobe projector flashed images of the performers on a giant screen at the back of the stage. Everything was on the wrong scale. I moved out.

By the time I got to the operations trailer with my cashier's checks I was a little less shaken. I dropped the checks with one of Wes's men and headed back up Hurd Road toward 17B and White Lake.

Back at the office things were beginning to slow down a bit. Most of the local citizenry had apparently gone to bed, their shotguns by their pillows, no doubt. Missing-person phone calls and demands for supplies had almost ceased, and the staff had thinned out. The clock on Wes's desk read just after midnight. I tried to think of things that I might have forgotten to do. "Anybody heard from the Tose Truck?" I asked.

Then the Sheriff called.

Bethel's Finest

The Telephone Building, White Lake, New York
Saturday, August 16, 1969, 12:40 A.M.

Joel hangs up the phone and stares at it blankly for several seconds. He then looks around the room as though he were a camera making a slow horizon scan. After his gaze has traversed about a hundred and eighty degrees, John, face haggard, cigarette in mouth, checkbook open in front of him, notices the vacant eyes.

"Joel?"

At first there is no response. Then, out of what seems to be a different dimension in time, comes a perfectly casual "What?"

"Who was that you just spoke to?"

There is another long pause. "What? Oh." Joel rubs his eyes. "That was the Sheriff. He says he's got the traffic turned around at the Quickway exit and he needs someone to tell the people they're not going to get in."

John frowns. "Someone to tell them they're not going to get in! Christ! Why can't his men tell them they're not going to get in?"

"I don't know. I guess they won't believe what cops tell them. He said he needs someone in authority from the Festival to tell them."

"Who the fuck has any authority around here any more? Except to sign checks. Tell him to use his loudspeaker, or his command voice . . . or his kazoo. Shit! We don't have enough to do, we have to play policeman."

"What?" Joel says. "Oh yeah. Right. No. If he needs our help—if he thinks he needs our help—to get people headed back toward New York, well, he needs it. Or whatever. Christ! I don't know. I'll take my bike and go over."

John squints over his cigarette, says nothing, returns to his checkbook.

Joel walks outside and mounts his motorcycle. The night is cool and humid.

Strictly speaking, there is no road. There is only an enormous maze of cars twenty or thirty yards across stretching away in the darkness to the east. Joel maneuvers his cycle through the metal hulks for several miles, thinking to himself that the scene suggests the recent passage of a giant saltshaker with car-sized holes. Then, too, there is the eerie stillness, the end-of-the-world hush lying incongruously over all these lifeless machines.

Outside Monticello the stillness disintegrates rapidly; first with the low thrum of idling motors, then, nearer the Quickway, with the angry snarl of revving engines. Voices can be heard, and an occasional loud honk. At the highway itself there is pandemic confusion, a clutter of people and automobiles reminiscent of Hieronymus Bosch.

As Joel approaches, he sees a single flashlight-wielding sheriff's deputy in the middle of the road, his shakily rigid façade of authoritarian dispatch imperfectly concealing the panic-stricken wounded animal underneath. He is fiercely waving on all westbound cars, not permitting them to exit, but after several minutes of observation it is clear to Joel that this tactic isn't working. Most vehicles, once waved on, are simply proceeding to the next exit, returning to the highway in the eastbound lanes, and then puttering merrily back to the unguarded exit opposite where the deputy is standing. There is a long line at that exit now.

Joel parks his motorcycle and walks over to the deputy.

"Listen," he says, "it's no good waving these cars on. We've got to get them turned around and headed back toward the city."

"Who the fuck are you?" the deputy inquires through clenched teeth.

"My name is Rosenman."

This apparently rings no bell. In fact, it only seems to connote an added irritation, another party heard from, more noise in the din.

"Get your ass over there to that squad car, Rosenman."

Joel complies.

A few minutes later, the deputy gets on his radio. "Sheriff? I got a . . . subject here. Says his name is Rosenman. He's . . ."

The radio jumps, or seems to. "Rosenman! Listen, goddammit, he's running the Festival and he gives the orders. You're under his instructions. You got that? You do what he tells you."

"Right!" says the deputy in a clipped efficient tone.

"Joel?" squawks the voice from the radio. "You hear what I said?"

"Yes, Sheriff. I heard."

"O.K. Well, I meant it. As far as I'm concerned, you and John are the law around here."

Joel stares at the radio.

"You receiving me, Joel?"

"Yes, Sheriff. I'm receiving you."

"O.K. Good luck."

"Well, Mr. Rosenman," says the deputy after a few moments, "I guess I better get busy."

"Right," says Joel, trying to get used to his new-found power, and hoping fervently that he won't find any more.

Joel on the Festival—II

I woke up scratching. It was still dark. My investigating hand encountered oddly elevated stretches of skin. I fumbled for the bed lamp, thought better of it, and eased out of bed. I turned on the light in the tiny bathroom of the motel cabin.

Then I saw them: red splotches all over my body, each splotch itching as if it were in competition with all the other splotches. Scratching frantically, I made a rough diagnosis: I had died during the night. Alternatively, I had hives. Something I ate? Something that was eating me? Put a corporal in a general's uniform and he gets hives—and medals. Overcome with sympathy for myself, I took a twelve-hour antihistamine cold capsule and switched off the bathroom light. Outside, the dawn of the second day of the Festival was tingeing the horizon.

A couple of hours later, just as the rain that had been trying to start all morning really got going in earnest, I got up and headed off back to the front. Some of the rain quickly leaked into the viscera of my Honda, and it gasped and died in midjourney. I spotted the Diamond Horseshoe up the road and wheeled my motorcycle's carcass up to its driveway.

The Diamond Horseshoe was a once-popular resort hotel that had fallen on hard times along with the rest of the White Lake area. Maintenance had finally dropped below legal standards, and the place had been condemned. Then along came Woodstock Ventures with a huge staff to house and an offer that the owners of the old hotel couldn't refuse. They made a desultory attempt to clear up the safety hazards in the place, tried to reintroduce a water supply, mostly cold, and settled on an exorbitant monthly rental. By and large, however, the staff members who lived there, mostly sublieutenants and underlings, loved it. Even after a fire had broken out one night, they refused to take up residence anywhere else. Some of them acted as self-appointed cooks, and there was a huge communal dining room where everybody took their meals both before and during the Festival. There weren't quite enough bedrooms to go around, so many people slept on couches in the living room, or in sleeping bags wherever there was an open space.

I was struck by how run down the place was inside. Of course, "run down" was synonymous with "funky," and this contributed greatly to the Diamond Horseshoe's appeal. A sleepy construction-crew member offered me some breakfast. I declined and asked for a phone. They were probably wondering about me over in White Lake. He indicated its location and said that it had been working only on occasion. This turned out not to be one of them.

Cut off from communications and exhausted by the effects of the cold capsule, I sank into a tattered overstuffed armchair and waited for my motorcycle to dry. As I sat, the hotel came to life around me. Long-hairs indistinguishable from those who were filing toward the Festival or from those I had seen massed in the performance area began to assemble in the living room and the dining area. Many of them said hello to me without having met me. There was a casual friendliness in the air that made me even drowsier, and as the rain let up outside, I dropped off to sleep.

A half hour later I woke up, startled by my surroundings. The sun had come out; a good omen for my Honda. Sure enough, a running start down the driveway was sufficient to get me chugging along 17B once again. Back to work.

The shoulder of the road was filled with hikers. Some of them had been trekking for hours, having abandoned their cars miles before. But they were determined not to miss the Festival. Closer to White Lake, I passed the outermost of the parking lots. Here mud was the predominant décor. I noted that where we had planned to have neat rows of cars arranged on the basis of so many square feet per vehicle, there were instead fields full of colorful camper-trailers and tents—all randomly placed amid the slime.

At the White Lake office it was business as usual, if by usual you understand five frantic phone calls per minute, ten crises per hour, and snap decisions at some undetermined but ulcer-producing rate. When I arrived, Jock was so snowed under that only the point on the top of his head was visible. He inquired as to where the hell I had been. I answered him with a friendly if emphatic gesture and turned to Lee Mackler, who was proffering phone messages by the dozen. Some kids had savagely attacked a water main, cutting off part of our supply. Abruzzi had been calling for more medical assistance. I was informed that we had broadcast a request for doctors and nurses to come to La Guardia Airport, where a chartered plane would be waiting to carry them up to White Lake. Thousands responded to the appeal; five or six doctors and nurses among them.

Accounts of the Festival in the media were growing more numerous by Saturday afternoon, and, not surprisingly, they tended to harp on our one-of-a-kind traffic jam. At that time, Woodstock's news value still depended on a motionless bunch of cars.

The pace in the office picked up as the show started again in the afternoon. Helicopters once again became primarily important. Performance schedules were changing all the time as the acts played indeterminately longer sets. Making sure that the performers were transported to and from the stage was a job that kept several helicopter dispatchers busy full time.

The strain of dealing with the performers was felt in other quarters, too. Artie himself was under considerable pressure. Periodically he would call the office from a phone near the stage and demand thirty cases of Coca-Cola or a gross of Q-tips. He was not a man to slight the amenities just because of a crisis or ten. After a while I took to placing the receiver on my desk whenever he phoned and attending to business until I estimated it was time to say "It's already gone down." Then I would hang up.

Late in the afternoon someone noticed that we hadn't heard from the medical group for a long time. They were still shorthanded, a telephone call revealed, and I decided to go out there to see if we couldn't round up some more volunteers. It was a thin excuse to get out of the office for a little while.

I stopped at the motel for a windbreaker since by now everybody expected either a chilly evening or rain or both. I was coming out of our cabin when I caught sight of Renee, strolling around the grounds clutching our massive corporate checkbook to her ample corporeal bosom. She complained that some longhairs had ventured onto motel property looking for something to drink and had frightened her. I could tell that she disapproved of the disorder that was the hallmark of the weekend. She asked me if I wanted to see the checkbook, and I politely said yes, although I didn't actually give a damn what the balance was. I already knew that it had to be negative enough to make strong men weak. Renee's impeccable script was, in the most recent entries, neater than ever. Everything was in order. I suspect that by being so neat about our accounts, Renee hoped she could somehow tidy up the whole Festival morass. I told her not to worry, that in spite of appearances things were pretty much under control. This blatant nontruth comforted her. I relieved her of the latest batch of cashier's checks for the NYC cops and resumed my journey to the site.

That which had blown my mind the day before now

seemed a fact of life. There was a medium-size city on Max Yasgur's dairy farm. It had always been there.

After dropping off the salary checks, I drove over to the field hospital to see what I could do. The condition of our medical services appeared to be excellent. There were a great many first-aid cases wandering about, but treatment seemed to be more prompt here than in most New York City hospitals—no great commendation, to be sure, but under the circumstances . . . After a few minutes of standing around feeling useless, I decided to go back to the office.

At the intersection of Hurd Road and 17B, on some impulse, I turned right and drove west. It turned out to be the smartest thing I had done all weekend. In less than a mile of curves and gentle hills, the Festival disappeared completely. I rounded a bend and saw a beautiful cottage situated precisely on the edge of a little lake not more than a hundred yards from the road. A family of four was having dinner out on the sun deck, oblivious to what lay to the east of them. There were no cars, no long-hairs, no music. Even the mud had disappeared. I was astonished that such antithetical worlds could coexist so close together. But how much time, I asked myself, could a man with my sense of duty spend on such a scene when there was vital work to be done elsewhere? Centuries. I struggled free of temptation and sped back to pandemonium.

I was cheerfully received back in the trenches at the Telephone Building. Things seemed to be going well. The acts were being hustled smoothly on and off the stage. The kids weren't misbehaving. The weather was almost clement. Apart from the exhaustion that was by now running rampant among the staff, nothing was seriously amiss. I suddenly remembered that I had not seen or heard anything about the Tose truck all day. I was told that it had managed to get off 17B and was making its way toward the site along some little-known back roads. I secretly doubted that any of the back roads east of the site were little known any more, but I had to admit that that Tose truck driver was one plucky fellow.

That night we attempted to keep our helicopter shuttles

running far later than we had the night before. This attempt had to be co-ordinated with an effort to rig up a makeshift heliport at the site, complete with landing lights. Our resident electrical genius, Chris Langhart, was given the assignment after the electricians of record said it simply couldn't be done in the time available with the materials at hand. There was some urgency in finding a solution, since no less a personage than Lenny Kaufman was already air-borne, and the pilot of his chopper had suffered a loss of tachometer function on his previous trip, the tach being the key instrument for determining whether one's helicopter is going up or down. Lenny told me later that it was already dark when they came in over the site, and there was no landing area visible. They were contemplating a ditch when our instant heliport suddenly became a blaze of light. "Over there!" yelled Lenny, and the pilot brought her in.

Langhart's solution had been to affix hundreds of light bulbs to the fence surrounding the landing pad and then simply plug in the fence. It took a few security guards to prevent people from engaging in any ill-advised leaning, but the choppers flew far into the night.

As the evening wore on with still no major incidents, I permitted myself a canapé of optimism. Maybe the worst was over. Then again, maybe the worst was yet to come.

New York State's Finest

The Telephone Building, White Lake, New York
Saturday, August 16, 1969, 12:05 P.M.

John comes cascading into the room where Joel and a dozen or so staff members are milling around at cross-purposes.

"Joel! Joel!" he shouts, rushing past his partner into the center of the room. "Where the hell is he?"

The staff looks at him anxiously. A lot of freaking out has been going on. Joel taps him on the shoulder, and he wheels around.

"Joel, for Christ's sake, where were you? We've been rescued!"

Now it is Joel's turn to look anxious. "Rescued?"

"Ratner just got the word over his radio. Some higher-up in the State Police is on his way to take over."

Joel's face breaks into a huge smile. He throws back his head. "Ya-hooo!" he says, grabbing John around the waist and jumping up and down.

The two of them careen around the room while the staff members shrink back and hug the walls.

"Where? When?" says Joel.

"They're on their way, he said."

"Well, let's be outside to meet them, man!"

They break for the door. Outside, they sprint over to the Sheriff's patrol car and come to a skidding stop just next to the driver's seat. The Sheriff is bent over, talking on his radio.

"What's the latest?" John asks.

The Sheriff puts down his transmitter with a shaky hand. "They're on the way. They're taking the back road from Ferndale and they should be here any minute now."

Joel runs down the street to see if he can catch a glimpse of them approaching. John stands on tiptoe and scans the horizon impatiently, keeping an ear cocked for any further transmissions. He feels profoundly relieved. The State Police will end the Festival, disperse the crowd, ward off all the catastrophes, riots, stampedes, and explosions he has been expecting to occur at any moment. The hour of deliverance is at hand. Blessed be the State Pigs.

Joel comes tearing back up the street. "I see them! I see them!" he says, pointing in several different directions.

The Sheriff bursts out of his car, knocking John over as he opens the door. "Where?" he shouts, moving toward Joel and tripping over John's ankle.

"Over there, for Christ's sake," Joel answers, pointing more precisely.

John and the Sheriff pick themselves up and look in the direction Joel has indicated. Three flashing red lights can be seen about half a mile distant, and soon sirens can be heard. It is a convoy of three police cars, crawling painfully through the massed traffic. When they are about three hundred yards away, someone jumps out of the middle car and begins striding purposefully toward the middle of town. He is immediately joined by two uniformed figures. As the trio gets nearer, Joel and John can see a husky man with an impossibly tiny crew-cut head flanked by state troopers with their palms on the holstered butts of their prominent .45s. All three look grim and determined.

The tiny-headed man approaches. He is wearing a short-sleeved white shirt and a black string tie. Deliverance comes in strange shapes.

"Roberts? You Roberts?" he asks Joel.

"I'm Roberts," John volunteers readily.

"Where's Rosenman?"

"Right here, sir. Boy, are we ever glad to see you."

"Right," says the man, exuding cool efficiency. "Now look, I've just come straight from Albany, so what I'm telling you is one-hundred-percent official."

Joel and John lick their chops.

"Here's the scoop. My men and I have been ordered to put ourselves completely at your disposal. You just tell us what you want us to do to help keep things going smoothly, and we'll do our best to comply."

Joel and John stare at him with their mouths open.

"That's official, boys," the man says, confident that he is giving them comfort. "We're in your hands."

No one seems to appreciate the humor in the situation.

Joel on Charlie's Cashier's Checks

We were certainly up to our ears very early on. The State Police had made the difficult decision to close off access, which actually wasn't such a difficult decision given the condition of the roads. Highway 17B was a traffic dispatcher's nightmare. The fairgoers had hit it first because it was the logical route from the Quickway to the Festival site. After 17B coagulated, the resourceful long-hairs began to seek out secondary, tertiary, quaternary, and quinary roads in the area, and very quickly there was no way to get from hither to yon except by helicopter.

Between one and two million people made a move toward the Festival that weekend, and the roughly half million who made it were there for the duration, like it or not. It was the possibility that they might not like it, and might not like many other things, including each other, that made me a trifle hysterical on the subject of "keeping the peace."

I don't like to admit it, since it's so contrary to the Woodstock image, but right from the start I was flat-out paranoid about having all those kids as our house guests for the weekend. Every time terrified parents or irate Citizens Committees came pounding on our door with their grievances, I would hang back, secretly agreeing with them. Even after their fears had been calmed by the silver-tongued Michael or the fork-tongued Artie, I, the promoter, remained profoundly uneasy. I thought the weekend was going to be a holocaust somehow. I don't know why. I had no idea that we were going to get so many people. As a matter of fact, I was sure we weren't even going to sell enough tickets to break even. I guess it was just a neurotic fear on my part that no matter how small the crowd, there would be some primitive outbreak of violence that would smear Woodstock across the history books and the court dockets of New York State.

Starting off so uneasy made me very susceptible to panic when our audience turned out to be ten times larger than expected. I forsook all humanity at once. I wanted Doberman pinschers. I wanted free-fire zones and electrified barbed wire. I wanted helicopter gunships and machine-gun emplacements.

Fortunately, I was not the only one responsible for crowd control. If I'd been calling the shots alone during those first few hours, the National Guard would have come dropping out of the sky so fast that the heads' heads would have been spinning. Talking to Wes and Jock and one or two other knowledgeable people though, convinced me that the immediate application of as much power and voltage and napalm and shrapnel as possible would not be in the best interests of our cause. After some thought, we adopted a less militaristic solution.

Our major worry was what the kids were going to do with all their free time when the stage wasn't alive with rock bands. The best way of dealing with that was to eliminate the free time, to rock around the clock, in other words, and hope that the nonstop entertainment would keep the kids riveted to their seats, or their mud puddles, or whatever. It was obvious—and beautiful.

The only hitch was that we had to convince all the groups and their business managers that our solution was the best for all concerned. Luckily, some of them were so thrilled to be there that they jumped at the chance to get back up on the stage a second time or extend their original set. After all, we had what appeared to be the largest live audience that any musician had ever played to. Some other groups just plain refused to play any more than their contracts called for, and that was fair enough, I suppose. Oh, we moaned and groaned about how we were in a crisis and how they sort of owed it to the kids to play just a little longer and so forth, but if they still refused, we didn't sink our teeth into their ankles as they were walking away. Enough people were co-operating so that we could get along without them.

Then we approached the Grateful Dead, but to understand their position you have to know how one contracts for the services of a rock-music group.

Normally, one negotiates the terms of a performance contract with the group's business manager. His job is to make sure (1) that all the terms of the contract are such that the group can live up to them, and (2) that the performance conditions are such that the group will not suffer unusual hardship in the process of fulfilling its obligations. In addition, the business manager must ascertain the financial solidity of the person he is negotiating with in order to make sure that his group is going to get paid what is due them.

Once the terms of a contract are agreed upon, it is signed and filed with the musicians' union. Then fifty percent of the group's fee is paid by the promoter to the business manager as a binder and an advance; the other fifty percent is paid once the group performs.

It's the fifty-percent split that causes the burns. Groups, being somewhat unreliable, occasionally do not show up at the appointed time and place. Conversely, promoters, being the scoundrels that they are, present company excluded, have been known to vanish with the ticket receipts just before a group gets off the stage. As a result, many business managers have become justifiably wary and demand a check as their acts get up to play.

None of this was news to us, and we were prepared to hand the managers their second fifty percent just prior to performance time. The trouble started when they started to get nervous.

We should have guessed that it would be a problem. We knew what a good manager's function was. Still, it shocked me.

The Grateful Dead was a group that was superpopular with the kids thanks to their free concerts and their funky don't-give-a-shit-about-material-possessions attitude. But when I called their manager and asked him if they would mind playing a little longer than their contract required, I found that he did not share his clients' philosophy.

"You guys in trouble?"

"Not at all," I replied.

"I mean bread trouble."

"Of course not. It's just that we have too many people for the facilities and we don't want to have them roaring around getting into trouble because the stage is dark. Now are you guys gonna play another set or what?"

"We're not gonna play at all, man."

"WHAT?"

"You heard me. You guys are in some kind of trouble, and we're not going on stage without our money."

"Without your money? Without your money? What the fuck are you talking about? You'll get your money just like everybody else."

"How's that?"

"By check, when your boys go on."

"Not good enough."

"Not good enough! All the acts are being paid that way!"

"Fuck the other acts. We want cash. You guys are in some kind of trouble, and I'm here to make sure the Dead don't get burned."

I didn't have enough problems; I was dealing with some sort of anticremation fanatic. "Cash," I shouted. "Where the hell do you expect me to get cash at 1:00 A.M. on a Sunday morning in the middle of Sullivan County?"

"That's your problem."

I would have counted to ten if I'd had the time, but I contented myself with three. "Listen," I said. "Forget the whole thing. Forget I called. You guys just play your normal set and . . ."

"Bullshit!" came the response. "You want us to go on, you get us that second fifty percent in cash or a certified check. Otherwise *you* can forget the whole thing."

He hung up on me.

I called John Morris, our stage manager, and asked him what he thought it would do to the line-up if the Dead didn't perform.

"The crowd'll tear us to pieces," he pronounced without hesitation.

Well, at least that narrowed the options. Somewhere I had to get my hands on $7,500.

The phone rang. It was the manager of the Who, who had just finished talking to the manager of the Dead and wanted me to know that his group wouldn't play without cash or a certified check either.

This was getting to be scary. Every group up there would be demanding cash soon if the word got around.

"Look, man," I said, improvising frantically, "we've got just enough cash to pay you and the Dead up front, but if this gets around to the other groups, everybody's just gonna have to be satisfied with a check." I slammed down the receiver, hoping the gesture would reinforce what I'd said and give the guy an excuse for letting his natural greed take over. I heard later that he raced right over to the manager of the Dead and taped his mouth shut.

So now it was $15,000.

Being a sprawling, highly diversified show-business conglomerate, Woodstock Ventures had established financial relations with many banks and opened numerous accounts in their various branch offices. Even as I was concluding my conversation with the manager of the Who, one of our favorite local bankers, Charlie Prince, was turning over in his bed, sound asleep in his cozy house filled with family and dogs. A placid Sunday at home stretched ahead of him, thanks in good part to the fact that there was a total traffic jam even as far away as Fallsburg, which was where Charlie Prince lived.

Charlie had worked his way up in the hierarchy of the Sullivan County National Bank from assistant teller to branch manager. He was as honest, hard-working, and co-operative as anyone could have been. During the difficult weeks of construction preceding the Festival, he had trusted John and me and extended to us the facilities of his bank without hesitation. He had a lovely family, and altogether the experience of meeting him was one of the few bright spots I can look back on.

The phone rang for about two minutes before Mrs. Prince picked it up. "Hello?"

"Hello, Mrs. Prince, this is Joel Rosenman over at the Festival. We've run into a problem and I think Charlie is the only person who can help us."

"Wait just a moment, Joel. I'll get him."

"Thanks a lot, Mrs. Prince. I'm awfully sorry to disturb . . ."

"Don't you worry about that," she said, bless her. "I know you boys have your hands full. Now hold on."

Another minute passed, during which I tried to estimate the chances that there was any way that Charlie could help.

"Joel?" It was the voice of a man trying to sound more awake than he was.

"Charlie? Look, I'm awfully sorry about calling you at this hour, but we're in kind of a bind, and the only thing I could think of was to call you." I launched into a capsule summary of the problem, emphasizing the fact that the groups' managers were in no mood to negotiate.

I waited. Charlie didn't say anything for a while. I took that as a good sign.

"Well, I sure see the problem," he said finally. "But I don't know what I can do about it."

I took that as a bad sign.

"I was afraid of that, Charlie. But isn't there any cash at the bank we could write you a check for? Or maybe some certified checks? I mean, I know it's late, but maybe if you came to the bank . . ."

"It's not that, Joel. I'd go to the bank in a minute if there was anything I could do there. But there isn't. We lock everything up in the vault on Friday afternoon, and it's on a time lock. Even if you know the combination, you can't open it till Monday morning."

"Do you lock up the checks, too," I asked, knowing in my guts that they did.

"Everything. The cash, the certified checks, the cashier's . . . Wait a minute!"

It was like a goddamn movie script.

"What? What?"

"Hold it a second. Give me a minute."

I held it a second. I gave him a minute.

Then, at last: "This is a real long shot, Joel, but I think we might have left the cashier's checks out by mistake."

"Oh, *All Right!* Charlie baby! Fantastic!"

"Now don't get all excited. I said it was a long shot. It's just that I put those checks in a different drawer Friday morning and I don't remember putting them back in the drawer that went into the vault at the end of the day."

"We're saved! We're saved!" I shouted. I didn't give a damn; I was going to get all excited.

"Now calm down, Joel. Even if they're in that drawer, I don't know how I can get to them. I mean, it just occurred to me that I couldn't make it through on a bicycle, the roads are so jammed up."

"Don't you worry about that, Charlie, my boy. Just grab your keys and await your own personal helicopter. I'll be right back to you."

One thing I had down pat by that time was arranging for helicopter transportation. Within two minutes I was calling Charlie back for directions.

"Now don't forget to call me as soon as you get to the bank," I said as we ended our conversation.

"Don't worry. I won't," he replied, adding excitedly after a moment, "Wow! That was quick. I can hear the helicopter coming. Be talkin' to ya." And he was gone.

So there I was waiting again. Always waiting right in the middle of the worst moments. Nothing much was going on at that hour of the morning in White Lake. There was a little chatter on the short wave, but otherwise things were quiet. Lee Mackler wandered in sleepily and asked if I wanted some coffee.

"No thanks, Lee. I'm wide awake."

"Yeah, I noticed that. What keeps you so alert?"

"Fear, same as everybody else."

"Funny. You're scared. John's scared. And Michael and Artie are up on the stage having the time of their lives. How come they're not scared?"

"I dunno, Lee. Maybe Jock and I are scared enough for the four of us."

The phone rang.

I let it ring again and then ripped it off its cradle. "Hello!"

"Hello, Joel? It's Charlie."

"Ah, Charlie," I said, "how kind of you to phone."

"I'm in the bank, Joel. Phew! That was some ride!" I got the impression he planned to go home via surface transportation. "Now I haven't even checked the drawer yet, Joel. Keep your fingers crossed."

There was a clunk as he put the phone down. I could hear his footsteps as he made his way over to where the checks might have been overlooked thirty-six hours before.

"Be there. Be there. Be there," I was chanting to myself.

Then I heard a "Yeeeeaahooo!" and after a second Charlie was screaming into the phone, "I got 'em, Joel! I got 'em!"

"Stay right there, Charlie," I screamed back. "Ah'm a'comin' right over."

I asked Lee to cover for me and moved out. Outside the office building, the night air was cool and unruffled. I got on my motorcycle and headed off toward the bank. As ever, the pressure having eased a bit, I felt an unaccountable depression. This time, however, I was able to console myself. In a few moments, after all, I would be in the Sullivan County National Bank, swapping checks after hours with a Prince.

John on the Festival—II

The phoning and co-ordinating continued unabated all through the early hours of Saturday morning. Occasionally, we would get calls from people at the site rhapsodizing over the performances, the behavior of the crowd, or the quality of the sound systems. Other calls were not so rhapsodic: reports of drug overdoses, good acid, bad acid, clean water, dirty water, food shortages, food wastages, etc. Wes, John Fabbri, Lee Mackler, and I made up a rotating team of problem solvers. We were joined throughout the night by assorted organizational and nonorganizational stragglers who would wander in for some warmth and coffee and then stay to answer phones.

At around 3:00 A.M., the calls from frantic parents started to roll in. The word on the enormity of the Festival had gone out, and the consensus of the media in their early reports was that a better-than-average catastrophe was in progress. I guess that it took until the wee hours Saturday for America's hysterical mothers to get America's indifferent fathers to *do* something, George, for heaven's sake!—and our procedure was to point out that despite all the reports to the contrary, everything was calm, the concert was progressing, the crowd was peaceful, and the facilities for eating, drinking, and defecating were sufficient. "Your child's all right, sir," we would conclude. "He's no worse off than if he were on, say, a camping trip." "*I* know that," the harassed male voices would respond, "but would you please tell him to for Christ's sake call home. His mother is going bananas here." We promised to do what we could, but we also mentioned that there were only a few pay phones at the site to serve roughly half a million people. At this point, the mothers, who were invariably listening in, would scream something like "My baby! He'll be trampled to death!" and we would have to go through the whole gamut of calming explanations yet a second time before finally disconnecting. Then, having made a note of the child's name, we would call the stage and ask them to announce that So-and-So should call home as soon as possible. That was the best we could do.

The atmosphere of high tension in the Telephone Building kept us all awake and functioning long past our normal exhaustion points. It was with considerable surprise, therefore, that I noticed a hazy dawn begin to insinuate itself over soggy little White Lake. My surprise was followed close on by an overwhelming weariness, and I announced that I was going to lie down for a few minutes. I collapsed on some blankets in a corner and slept.

I awoke about three hours later, at ten o'clock, feeling totally unrested and very edgy. Up at the site, fifteen hours of music had just ended, and most of the crowd was apparently sleeping or passed out, or something like that. It had begun to rain again, but the phones were silent.

Wes and John Fabbri catnapped at their desks and everyone else lay around in a stupor. Renee, however, was up and around. It was she, in fact, who woke me up. "John," she hissed, "there's someone here to see you, and I don't like the looks of him." Over near the door was a short, slight, balding fellow in his mid-forties, ill-clad and obviously terrified of our general ledger bookkeeper. I tottered over to him.

"Are you John Roberts?"

"Uh-huh."

"Are you authorized to accept papers on behalf of Woodstock Ventures?"

"Uh-huh."

"Then it is my duty to give you this," he said, and handed me our first summons and complaint.

"Thank you," I said myopically, and the little man scrambled for the door.

Gradually, I began to focus. The complainant was Monticello Raceway, and they were alleging that because we'd failed to provide adequate access to the Festival, most of their potential customers had been unable to reach the betting windows Friday night. They wanted $300,000 as compensation.

I called our attorney over in Liberty. "Do we have to do anything? Like, is there any particular sort of reply we're supposed to make?"

"Nah" was the answer. "Just put the damn complaint in your pocket along with all the other damn complaints that are going to be served on you this weekend. I'll take all of 'em off your hands on Monday." He snickered. "I guess you're going to need a pretty large pocket."

I walked outside to get some air. The streets looked like some stock Hollywood refugee footage, endless files of homeless war victims trekking along in utter confusion and bedragglement. Every now and then someone would come up to me and ask for a cigarette. No, he would tell me, he hadn't been to the site. He'd come for the music, but the crowd and the hassles had been too much to cope with, so he'd just fallen in with some other wanderers and sort of hung out. Now everybody was wet and tired and they were going home. No bitterness; no rancor; it had been a really heavy trip, a far-out scene. Enough was enough, though, and, for them, it was over.

I walked across the road to the delicatessen. The owner was a jovial old guy who was having the time of his life. He loved the kids—and the business, well, just look at the shelves. The only cloud in his sunshine was the fact that he couldn't get additional deliveries in until Monday, so he was going to be sold out at the height of demand. "I wish someone had told me in advance how big this thing was going to be," he lamented. I agreed that it would have been nice to know and bought a Twinky.

Back at the office the Sheriff was waiting.

People from everywhere were still trying to get to the Festival, people with Saturday and Sunday tickets, for example. Despite Joel's recent efforts, the Quickway was backed up for twenty miles, and the practice of abandoning cars on the roadway was beginning. Ratner felt that I had to go on the radio and tell people not to come. I called our attorney, who told me there was no way I could call off ticket holders. "But," I moaned, "ticket—no ticket; that's a finer distinction than the Sheriff is prepared to tolerate." He came right back at me: "How about refund—no refund? Are you prepared to tolerate that?"

Refunds! Jesus!

I told the Sheriff that I couldn't turn away people with tickets. "Goddammit!" he said, and then "Shit!" We finally agreed that he would let ticket holders off the Quickway but tell them there was no place to go except on foot. Meanwhile, I was to go on the radio and fend off potential gate crashers. I contacted a New York station and was on the air inside of a few hours. I delivered my prearranged spiel, and the Attorney General later used it against us. We gave refunds.

By noon the show had gotten started again, and we all got back to manning the phones. It was a big day. We had to find Canned Heat, Creedence Clearwater Revival, the Grateful Dead, Keef Hartley, Sly and the Family Stone, Janis Joplin, Jefferson Airplane, Mountain, Quill, Santana, and the Who, all of whom had large retinues and innumerable quirky demands to go along with them. They kept us hustling.

Around three I took a moment out to call my family. I got Billy on the line finally and explained the situation. He was curiously and reassuringly ambivalent. He could see we had financial hassles to contend with and it was clear that we were going to have quite a party at the Bank on Monday. But from where he was sitting, Woodstock wasn't looking so bad. We were beginning to get a good press, apart from the drug stories, and the general drift seemed to be that the promoters were struggling valiantly and selflessly to deal with all the problems. True, the problems were of their own making, but most of them were also unforeseeable. I thanked Billy for the comforting words and hung up, not particularly comforted.

The afternoon wore on. The phones rang and rang. The rain fell and fell. It was getting almost monotonous, but every time the tedium got vaguely restful, some nasty little irritant would bring me back to the contemplation of how much money I was losing. One time I answered the telephone and it turned out to be a woman reporter from some upstate paper. She offered her condolences on the weather. I thanked her and asked her to call back on Labor Day. This made her testy. "Don't you realize you're the mayor of the third-largest city in the State of New York? The press has a right to talk to you." "I'm a little busy running the third-largest city in the State of New York right now," I said. "Just tell me how you feel," she persisted. "Sullen," I responded. "Oh yeah? Well look, your Honor, you brought those locusts there and I hope they strip you clean." In my best mayoral fashion I made a loud rude noise into the phone and hung up.

Other reporters were less obnoxious. Most of them were pleasant and sympathetic, in fact. One was accompanied by a photographer who took some pictures of me, one of which later appeared in *Life*'s special edition on the Festival. I looked like a retarded troll.

Saturday's high point, in retrospect, was the arrival in White Lake of a friend of mine from college. He was accompanied by another Penn classmate of mine and a girl. Her name was Rona. "Is there any way we can be of help?" she asked. "No," I answered, "but will you be around in a few years, when I get out of jail?" She laughed. "Everything's going to work out," she said. "Believe me." For some strange reason, I did, and when things did work out reasonably well many months later, I married the lady. She can't sing a note.

As night drew on, rumors became rife. The word was that hunger-crazed crowds had fallen upon Max's prize bulls and devoured them. We were alerted to the possibility that a motorcycle gang might attack the stage with knives and chains. The radical underground had reportedly proclaimed Woodstock the birth of a nation and were now urging all and sundry to march on and liberate Monticello. There were also the genuine problems to contend with. Bad acid was sending dozens of kids on weird trips. Several attempts were made to "off" the food stands because they were allegedly charging exorbitant prices. We sent some of our renegade New York cops and some Hog Farmers to cool that down, much as we would have liked to see Joerger *et al.* offed, and the stands stood.

The radical underground, whatever proclamations they might have made, spent the greatest part of their time running around distributing literature of uncertain provenance. Their movement crested when Abbie Hoffman jumped on the stage to grab the microphone, and bottomed immediately afterward when a member of the Who kicked him off. The crowd just wasn't political. About the only burning issue I heard discussed all weekend was the hypothesis that Richard Nixon had seeded the clouds above our gathering in order to dampen the bodies and spirits of "the people," and it did indeed begin to rain late Saturday in earnest.

Joel on an Electrical Problem

Somehow it just didn't feel like Sunday in the Command Center. I had long since passed the point of physical and emotional depletion that physicians call death and was operating on pure zombie power. John Fabbri and Wes Pomeroy were falling asleep at their desks, having given up trying to work in shifts because of their terror that things would career out of control while they were off duty.

We had plenty to keep us busy. Helicopters had to be kept track of, as did a number of outraged—in all senses—local landowners who would have gone on the warpath if it hadn't been completely clogged with automobiles. Also, someone had to keep an eye on Jock, who cowered shamelessly in a corner with his checkbook and muttered, "This can't be happening. This can't be happening. . . ."

Of course it would be inaccurate to suggest that everything

had gone wrong up to that point. The State Police, by deciding to close off access to the Festival on Saturday, had kept the crowd down to a manageable half million. The rain, by falling heavily just during the hours when we weren't covered by rain insurance, had saved me from a lifetime of agnosticism. And we ourselves, we thought, by keeping our performers performing around the clock, virtually, had staved off a possible riot/catastrophe/group-grope. It was that decision, in fact, to keep the kids transfixed and pacific, that I was in the process of congratulating myself on when the worst phone call of the Festival—and my life—came through.

I remember it was John Fabbri who answered. The ex-Police Chief of South San Francisco ("The Industrial City") was, to coin a phrase, a bull of a man, one of those supercompetent operatives we'd been lucky enough to hire along with all the dunderheads. Even before he picked up the phone, he had been looking a little the worse for wear, hardly a surprising condition under the circumstances. He had gone through every harrowing incident of the previous seventy-two hours without a break in his stride or a quaver in his voice, so when his face took on the color changes of a traffic signal, red to yellow to green, I knew that trouble of an entirely different order was being brought to his attention.

"What is it, John?" I asked.

"I think we better get ourselves over to the stage area," he answered in a voice so strained that I barely recognized it.

"What the hell's gone wrong?"

"That was the stage electrician," he began, rising from his desk and heading for the door. "He says all the rain has washed away the dirt that was covering the main feeder cables, and it's starting to rain again. He says the crowd walking on the exposed cables has worn away the insulation."

He paused to try to get his breath. I'd heard enough to know what he would say next, however.

"He says that with all those kids being drenched and packed together the way they are, if the insulation goes, we're going to have a mass electrocution."

It had been two years since I'd given up cigarettes, but at that moment I lit up a Camel. I probably could have smoked a real camel and not known the difference. Fabbri was almost out the door.

"Where are you going, John?" I needed his advice now— more than ever, as the saying goes.

"We've got to get over to the stage."

"What for?" I asked, shaken by the realization that even his unshakeable composure had been overridden by adrenaline. "What the hell can we do over there?" He was so scared that I began to get a grip on myself. "What does the electrician want us to do?" I shouted into his face, grabbing his lapels to make sure I didn't lose him.

"He wants us to shut down for a while."

"We can't. We'll have half a million kids running around at loose ends."

"I know that, dammit," he yelled, breaking loose. "Now let's get out to that stage!"

He moved for the door again, and again I grabbed his coat. I sensed in him a crazy conviction that he could solve the insoluble if only he could get to the site of it and apply the force of his personality in time. He was a lot bigger than I was, and I was having a hard time restraining him.

"John!" I said as imperatively as I could. "There's nothing you can do out at the stage. The electrician'll do whatever we tell him to. That's why you've got to stay here and help me."

That, or my fingernails digging into his arms, seemed to bring him to his senses, but now that he was rational again, what the hell could he say? We could choose to keep the power running through those deadly cables and hope that the crowd wouldn't remove what was left of their insulation or we could shut down and hope that the crowd wouldn't go out of control. Either way we chose, a real tragedy could be the result, and John was simply stymied.

So was I, but I had the responsibility.

After about ten hellish rat-in-a-corner minutes, during

which no disasters occurred, I made up my mind and called the electrician.

"This is Rosenman," I said, hoping that would mean something to a guy who was used to taking his orders from Michael. "I want those stage lights kept on. I want that music running continuously. You understand?"

"Yessir," he said. "I read you loud and clear. But maybe you didn't hear about the cables. . . ."

"I know all about the cables," I spat back at him, "but I don't want that music to stop for a moment. Isn't there any way for you to switch off those cables without darkening the stage?"

"I've been thinking about that, actually," he replied. "I could run everything from some protected lines, but it'll take me a while to work out the linkage."

"You work out the switchover as fast as you can," I said, "but make the change without losing one minute of music. Is that clear?"

It was.

I could tell from the look on Fabbri's face that he disagreed, but I was pretty sure I would have seen the same look if I'd decided the other way. Either decision was wrong.

I don't remember much about the next hour. I don't remember who entered or left the office, or whether I dealt with any other things, or . . . much of anything at all. All I remember is my smoking a lot of Fabbri's Camels while he sat motionless in his chair, and waiting for the lights to dim like they used to when the switch was pulled on Jimmy Cagney.

I was twenty-six years old. I knew that there were plenty of men my age and younger, in the Army or the Marines, for instance, who were responsible for other people's lives, but I didn't see how anyone could be competent to make such decisions. I certainly didn't feel that I was, and I sat immobilized that long, long hour and waited for the electrician to call me back.

Finally he did. "It's O.K.!" he shouted. "I've made the switch. The exposed cables are dead now."

"Does the stage have power?" I asked.

"It's hummin' away with power to spare."

I looked over to Fabbri and gave him the thumbs-up sign. He slumped forward onto his desk, too tired to be relieved.

"That's terrific!" I said to the electrician. "That's absolutely fantastic! You did great. Keep up the good work."

We hung up and I lit another Camel. It seemed that I had started smoking again in earnest.

John on the Festival—III

Sunday seemed like a day of perpetual night. It began with frantic phone calls to the helicopter landing platform, where Chris Langhart's lights had suddenly gone out. Landing in wet darkness near half a million tightly packed bodies was not a procedure sanctioned by the FAA. Improvisation was called for, and a flashlight brigade was formed to bring down the choppers until something more permanent could be devised. Thus thwarted, the Higher Being gave our lights back to us and retired to His workshop to think up more torments. Around dawn He was back, this time with a downpour in earnest: angry, determined, and decidedly drenching. It wasn't one of your stop-start affairs, but an uninterrupted torrent that turned the performance area into a muddy river delta. It went on and on implacably until dusk and, as Joel has related, almost resulted in a mass electrocution.

There were more prosaic anxieties as well. We came into our second lawsuit, brought by one Jud's Riding Stables, which was overrun by long-hairs out for a gallop. The stables were about a quarter of a mile from the stage, and, given the size of the crowd, that meant they were effectively part of the site. All weekend the horses were mounted, bareback, and exercised extensively. The flower-child theory that animals are a part of nature and belong to everyone precluded paying Jud any money for the use of his steeds or even asking his permission. Jud, accordingly, looked to us for redress and demanded $300 compensation. In all my experience, before the Festival and thereafter, this was the only time I ever saw anyone ask to be recompensed only the amount he had lost. I wanted to give Jud $400, but we later settled for three.

Jud was by no means the only one of our neighbors to be overrun. They all were, and those who had refused to rent us their land when we asked them looked upon their wiser and wealthier fellow farmers and began to fester. How to recoup? Rumor was that the Festival was a financial bust, so suing later probably wouldn't serve any purpose. Conclusion? Get compensated now. Make the rascally promoters settle on the spot. Get a check from them.

Now we had been writing checks all weekend on the basis of the line of credit at the Bank, but even that deeply sunk well was in danger of drying up. I consulted with my family and we agreed that only those checks bearing directly on continuing the performance or on the health and safety of the crowd should henceforth be written. In addition, commitments of payment were to be curtailed as much as possible whether they involved a check or not. The only problem with this policy was my well-deserved reputation as an easy touch. I am incapable of not paying someone after I've told him I'm going to pay him, and I even have trouble telling people I'm not going to pay them in the first place, especially if they have reasonable grievances and seem likely to resort to violence. An important part of my duties became, therefore, the avoidance of money seekers. I was aided in this effort by the fact that whatever Judas had let it slip that I held the purse strings had not provided his listeners with my picture. My face was not well known in White Lake, unlike Michael's or Joel's, so I instructed our staffers to inform all angry locals and other geld hunters that I had already left for the city.

Everything went smoothly to begin with. I sat smugly at my desk while two or three would-be creditors not five feet away from me were told that I wasn't there. It was all I could do to suppress my giggles. Then a group of our angry farmer neighbors came tromping in and suppressing giggles no longer preoccupied me. Here were half a dozen good-size outdoor types, after all; people used to working with their hands, wringing things. And they were more than just a little p.o.'d. They growled about the indignities their acres and their families had suffered at the hands of our customers and wanted to know where that S.O.B. Roberts was, 'cause he was the man who was damn well going to see to it that they got repaid for all the damage. I sat there and smiled weakly, tch-tching and shaking my head as Renee listened to their complaints and told them of my absence in New York. They stormed around a little, but it looked like the game had been won. Then I chanced to look out the window, and who should I see coming toward me but Sheriff Ratner, a man who could have business with no one in that building except that S.O.B. Roberts.

"Whew!" I said. "Hot in here," and lurched jerkily toward the rear exit to cool off in the pouring rain. It took about five seconds for me to become thoroughly drenched. Inside, I could see the Sheriff surrounded by the wrathful farmers. Once, he turned inquiringly to Renee and I heard her say, "I *told* them. He went back to the city." His reply, not being a Renee utterance, was inaudible, but it was clear that he was upset. After some more unproductive milling about, the farmers started to depart, heading for, unfortunately, the nearest and rear exit.

"Kinda wet to be standing out here, ain't it?" one of them asked me.

"I needed some air," I said, feigning a few coughs.

"He's crazy," said another.

"Hell, they're all crazy around here this weekend," said a third, and they went off.

I sank back against the side of the building and took a few deep breaths. Then I went inside to inform Ratner that I was still around.

The incident with the farmers was indicative of the mental transition I was making from total concentration on the Festival per se to concern over its likely repercussions. Throughout the weekend I had lived from moment to moment, measuring tomorrows only in terms of upcoming performances and their attendant problems. Now the task of putting Humpty Dumpty together again began to dominate my thinking, especially since the largest fraction of Humpty Dumpty was me.

First on the agenda was the cleanup. I talked with Mel Lawrence and Max about this for a good part of Sunday afternoon, and we decided to begin the moment the Festival ended. There was a problem about cleaning land that we hadn't rented: would it be construed as a tacit admission that we accepted responsibility for what had taken place there? We didn't know, but we voted to go ahead anyway and let the chips fall when and if they fell. Our people on the stage gave out the word that volunteers for the cleanup would be very welcome, and hundreds responded, staying behind on Monday and lending a valuable hand. We hired one Milton Sardonia to do the heavy work, and it took him and his men the better part of a week to complete it. Their bill was $20,000, but they did an absolutely magnificent job, and I reckon that we got a bargain.

Another subject that preoccupied us was setting up a team of people to help kids who ended up with no way of getting home, whether because they'd blown their money, their chance of a lift, or, temporarily, their minds. There wasn't a whole hell of a lot we could do for them, but that which we could, we did.

The crowd was indeed dispersing. It had been trickling away all Sunday. Toward midnight "only" 150,000 people were still hanging on. The concert lasted another nine hours. Our last act, Jimi Hendrix, had been paid more than any other entertainer for performing: $36,000. He went on at 6:30 Monday morning and played to about 25,000 bone-weary souls. *Sic transit gloria mundi.* About the time he got finished, Joel and I were en route to the Bank.

Joel on the Festival—III

Sunday came on as a day to be reckoned with right from the start. It barrel-assed in around 2:00 A.M. with the Charlie Prince cashier's checks saga, which kept me going for so long that there was no point in my trying to get any sleep. Both Jock and I had begun to have the feeling that a sort of cosmic malign intelligence was trying, so far just short of successfully, to do us in. We grew familiar with the presence of this force and began to take it into account in our decision-making. On Sunday I tried to put myself in the shoes of this transcendent nastiness. I concluded that if I were bent on the destruction of Rosenman and Roberts, I'd realize that I was running out of time and strike soon. I no sooner arrived at this conclusion than our little drama with electricity commenced.

In addition to making mass electrocutions possible, the rain fouled up transportation badly. Every so often we would lose a helicopter. One of them would get out of short-wave range, forced down in a valley somewhere, and everyone would OMMMM until we heard from the pilot. Honda-riding was downright treacherous, making me wish I'd purchased a helmet after all. We feared that the rain might bog things down so much that the mass exodus that we were all longing for would become stalled in the mire. Finally it occurred to us that we had better co-ordinate all tow trucks in the area so that we could get the most cars on the road in the shortest amount of time.

In the early afternoon a reporter from *Newsweek* interviewed me. He asked for some special insights into what he referred to as "the Woodstock Phenomenon." I didn't know what he was talking about.

All through the day the thought that we might be leaving in the evening kept floating in front of me like an oasis. Whenever I had a few moments to daydream, I would torture myself with thoughts that something might come up that would force us to stay. I tried to make sure that there was a person assigned to every loose end, the goal being to spring myself clear of responsibilities. The more Jock and I talked, the clearer it became that we would be spending some time at the Bank on Monday. I didn't know how much, but at the time I was convinced that it had to be more enjoyable than time spent in White Lake.

The performance area, our natural amphitheater, had become a natural sump, or so it appeared around 11:00 A.M. Sunday. Sitting had become wallowing. A once well-shod group of Woodstock staffers had become a ragged band of irregulars, with towels wrapped around their feet in place of mud-rotted shoes. Down by the stage I watched the police and the Woodstock security men subdue a burly youth who had been hanging by his hands, naked, from the elevated walkway leading from the stage to the performers' pavilion. Evidently he had swallowed a blue tab instead of a green one. He was positive that the cops were fire-breathing dragons. I made a mental note to supply them with Sen-Sen if we ever had another concert.

I bumped into Lenny—only figuratively, of course—who told me that just prior to being interviewed by the press, Artie had been seen smearing some dirt on his face. I thought that was precious. Another newsy item Lenny related concerned a particularly abrasive cop who had been handed an LSD-spiked Coke while directing traffic. Long after all automobiles in the area had congealed to a standstill, this hard-hat was still out on the road waving them on. Finally they led him away. I liked that story, too.

I went over to the medical area to deliver some checks to the ambulance drivers. In keeping with the spirit of the times, they had refused to drive any more unless they got their money. While I was there, a local cop apparently flipped out and started driving around the perimeter with his siren going "WOOP! WOOP! WOOP!" One of Lenny's guys informed him that unless he cooled it, the audience would be told that he was trying to frighten them. He cooled it.

For the most part, I should point out, the cops at the Festival were true gentlemen; the finest for real. They were polite, peaceful, industrious, and resourceful. Their performance turned a lot of people's heads around.

I came across Jim Mitchell after leaving the medical tent. He was stumbling around the operations trailer behind the stage and looked like he hadn't slept in several weeks. Jim was our man in charge of purchasing, and it turned out that he had left the site in a rage on Friday night after Artie had appropriated his trailer for himself and his family. When he had arrived at the trailer that evening, he discovered that the Kornfelds had moved in, leaving his belongings in a heap on the ground outside. He didn't say anything to anybody, because he's the kind of guy who bottles things up. He just up and went to New York City. Of course, as soon as he got there his conscience got the better of him. He turned right around and tried to make it back. He had finished his odyssey that morning, red-eyed and stoop-shouldered. I was glad to see him.

On my way out of the performance area I noticed that many fairgoers were heading in the same direction that I was. The exodus that we had been praying for had begun.

At 4:52 in the afternoon, the Tose truck arrived, paying $37.50 to one lucky poolster. The fifty thousand program books were piled up on a table along Hurd Road. They lasted about ten minutes. I never got one. Neither did Jock.

The arrival of the Tose truck didn't please everybody; Charlie Tuna, for example. Charlie Tuna was Artie's personal one-man publicity staff. He had tried to worm his way into the Woodstock apparatus by subverting some of the functions of the publicity and promotion operation, the responsibility for which he coveted. He grabbed me just before I got to the door of the Telephone Building. He had been standing out on the front lawn in the rain with a crumpled and soggy program booklet in his paw. He looked crestfallen.

"Er, hi, Charlie."

"Hi, guy. Ya seen the program book? A real bummer."

"A bummer? I thought they did a really good job."

"Oh, wow, man. I wouldn't have done that to you, man."

"What the hell are you talking about, Charlie? Done what?"

"Did you see the credits, man? What a bummer!"

I looked at the sodden page that he had opened to. There it was: Promotion—Sal Scaltro. The unkindest cut of all. For some reason, I apologized to him. He didn't deserve an apology, but the urge to say that I was sorry for something—for everything—had been growing in me all weekend.

The evening began to wind down. Over and over we checked out what still had to be done. Tow trucks were working like mad clearing the roads. The music was going smoothly on stage. Helicopter-dispatching was by now second nature. Jock and I glanced at each other. We were both ready to leave.

We wished everybody good luck for the hours that remained and promised to stay in touch. Then we left on a miraculously passable 17B. The police had done a truly commendable job in working out the traffic flow for the exodus. As we sped away from White Lake and our dwindling but still gargantuan Aquarian Exposition we were silent. Neither of us had any urge to look back.

AFTERMATH

John on the Bank—II

My first task on the Monday following the Festival was to go at once to the Bank. An eerie clairvoyance made me realize that they wished to see me. That and the bad publicity we'd gotten, the $800,000 we owed them that they knew about, and the fact that my hand had not stopped writing checks on their good name all weekend.

On my arrival, I went directly to my banker's office, there to face my banker, the Bank's lawyers, my lawyers, a bankruptcy contingent summoned by the Bank's lawyers, a bankruptcy contingent summoned by my lawyers, my brother Billy, various other bankers sent by the Bank to watch my banker, and a pet lizard that my rapidly aging banker kept in a large tank near his desk.

We quickly got down to business, which consisted entirely of one gargantuan unliened loan. The Bank wanted to know whether we would sign the lien instrument. My brother Billy came up with the $64,000 ($\times$ 12) answer by memorably and gallantly announcing that the Roberts family had (a) never been associated with a bankruptcy, (b) never welshed on a debt, and (c) didn't intend to spoil its record. After that it was all downhill. Two bankers fainted and the elderly banker himself took his first breath of the morning. The bankruptcy lawyers muttered darkly, gathered up their papers, handed out their cards in a gloomily skeptical manner, and left. The lizard and I eyed each other noncommittally. "That," said Woodstock's lawyer, "is possibly the most noble statement I have ever heard in my life." It was also one of the costliest, and the next hour was spent examining exactly what it entailed.

We ascertained that Woodstock owed in the neighborhood of $1,600,000.37. That amount would be diminished by monies still uncollected from our ticket outlets and from whatever the movie and the record album eventually brought in, if anything. The Roberts family agreed to secure the whole million plus by signing the lien against our trusts which had been negotiated in February.

It took the better part of a week for all the details to be ironed out. It was a week during which I spent the better part of every day down at the Bank with Renee going over the checkbook and trying to decide what was outstanding, what had yet to be written, and what, if written, should be stopped. It was a harrowing five days, largely because the Bank, sensibly enough, made an interim decision to hold payment on all checks until everything was straightened out. This resulted in a lot of longhair suppliers and laborers coming down to the Bank with their checks and demanding explanations. The third floor of the bank looked like Harvard Yard on the first warm day of spring.

While all this was happening, our ticket minions were scurrying about collecting receipts from the ticket outlets—those that would release the money—and carting the cash down to the Bank. Over the course of the week, some $300,000 arrived in greasy paper bags carried by Keith O'Connor. The arrival of this money was greeted by the Bank with mingled horror and joy: horror at the means of transport, joy at the arrival. Once at the Bank, a teller would be dispatched to count the stuff while two guards with pistols at the ready stood by.

Eventually all the papers were drawn and signed. Everyone was paid, and we all congratulated ourselves for weathering the crisis in a businesslike and honorable fashion. All except the lizard. He mostly slept.

Joel on the Aftermath

Since I was rather harried after the Festival, the few kindnesses that were shown me brought tears to my eyes. Jock has told of the magnificence of the Roberts clan in our hour of need, and my folks, too, were tremendously supportive. I kept in regular contact with them, one of the few times that, having recognized that they might be worried, I did something about it. They seemed to have a lot of confidence in me despite everything, and they frequently let me know about some of the pleasanter repercussions of the Festival. I remember one day particularly; after I had set some kind of a personal record by being named as defendant in three different suits, they called to inform me with pride that Woodstock had been included in the Encyclopaedia Britannica.

I think most of the people around me were awed by the enormity of what Woodstock had become, so that it was difficult for them to focus on the ghastly swarms of minutiae that made up the aftermath. It wasn't difficult for me though. The phone never stopped ringing, and we had four lines in those days. I let Renee handle as much of the incoming abuse as possible on the theory that she was already bananas and, therefore, had less to lose than this poor black-eyed pea. Fairly regularly, however, there was an ugly call that had to be taken by me personally, and these soon drove me deeper and deeper into depression and disarray. The Mafia seemed to be after me for some reason. Attorney General Lefkowitz kept summoning me to his office. The Bank turned us over to its "settlement department," and yet another law firm took up a stall in our stable of legal advisers, a firm that specialized in bankruptcies.

Woodstock had stirred the nation all right. There were about fifty or sixty thousand folks who had spent eighteen dollars for tickets which had only served to identify them as Thruway undesirables to the State Police. A fair percentage of these good people thought nothing of squandering one and sometimes as many as two message units on a call to Woodstock Ventures to talk over old times. Of course, it came as no surprise to me that they were out there, and after the Attorney General's sixth call (in the course of one of our slower mornings) on the subject, we decided to have a really serious discussion with each other about the whole problem. I opened the proceedings by suggesting that it would take a million dollars from somewhere to reimburse all the ticket holders who had been unable to get to the Festival. The meeting then adjourned, and Lefkowitz, realizing the impossibility of our raising anything like that kind of money, settled with us a few days later by consenting to drop the matter in return for our contributing $25,000 toward a partial reimbursement. At less than fifty cents a ticket, I counted that a bargain.

In addition to disappointed ticket holders, our neighbors up at the site kept regularly in touch with me. Most of them claimed that their land looked like it had been swept by hundred-fifty-pound locusts, insects notoriously incompetent with brooms. Fields had been flattened, I was told, fodder fouled, fowl barbequed, virgins deflowered, flowers depollinated, and so on. My way of dealing with these calls was to put them on "hold" and then casually mention to Jock that his fiancée was on the line.

But our most serious problems arose in connection with Michael and Artie. Like, they didn't dig being in debt, man. Bad vibes.

I could understand how they felt. My best guess at the time was that the company was a million five in the hole. So what did they suggest I do about it?

They were glad I had asked them that question. Their solution was for Jock and me to put our stock in escrow and personally guarantee the one-and-a-half-million debt, while they, together with two rancid music business leftovers, formed a new Woodstock corporation. The new company would exploit the Woodstock name, movie, record album, etc., and if and when it netted enough from the exploitation—after salaries, entertainment expenses, masseurs' fees, cigarette papers, cole slaw, and what-have-you were deducted—why then our escrowed stock would be released . . . into the deserving hands of their new partners.

"Hmmmm," I said. Even through the all-pervading stench of disaster, this deal smelled bad. It smelled so bad, in fact, that Jock and I called Michael and Artie a lot of bad names. They called us a lot of bad names back. We said they started it. They said their fathers were bigger than our fathers. Legal counsel was sought by all. War was declared.

Accountants call this a "corporate reorganization."

Relying on an unfortunate clause in our original contracts, Michael and Artie now refused to countersign any checks, guarantees, compromises, settlements, or anything until we made it worth their miserable whiles. This made some of our foremost creditors understandably tense—and only three of them were needed to throw us into bankruptcy. All our feeble proposals for an accommodation were brushed aside, and, as far as we could tell, we were really on the ropes. Then—enter Chuck Seton.

Tall, dignified, handsome, a renowned entertainment and publishing-business attorney, Chuck was already the lawyer for one of our employees. He was a man of fifty-nine who looked forty. When we got through with him, he had lost a great deal of his youthful vigor—and saved our hides.

I remember the night I met him because it was the same night that Jock and I confessed to each other that we had both been contemplating foregoing the use of an elevator on our next thirty-two-story trip to the street. We were having a laugh about that when our friend and ex-staffer John Morris called to suggest that I confer that very evening with a problem-solver who could really solve problems. I took his advice, and six hours later Chuck was telling me that unless he missed his guess—and he was a stranger to guess-missing—Jock and I had been holding all the cards all along without realizing it. Now if I would just follow this simple strategy . . .

Six backbreaking weeks of negotiation later, Michael and Artie were out of the company and Jock and I were on our way toward repaying Jock's family and putting our venture back on a solid footing. Our ex-partners had gotten $31,250 apiece, and we had gotten peace of mind.

Six months after that, they sued us for ten million dollars.

John on the Aftermath

On August 18 the situation was chaotic, desperate, and sad. The Festival had claimed a life. A man had been run over by a tractor while sleeping on the ground. Our cleanup director reported that there were probably other bodies in the woods. The deaths were a result of our actions, our three days of Peace and Music, our quest for profit. It turned out later that only the one man had died, and we were able to put that in perspective. Once you decide to carry on, you're more or less obliged to stop dwelling on your guilt feelings. It's an either/or proposition, I think, though it doesn't help my conscience any to think it.

Could we carry on? The corporation was broke. I was personally well over a million dollars in the hole. We still had enormous debts, and contingent liabilities in the form of lawsuits for negligence and property damage hung darkly over our heads. We had sold almost two million dollars' worth of tickets, and a case could be made for us giving all of that money back. Although we were a limited-liability company, there was ominous talk of piercing the corporate veil. There were criminal matters as well. The Sullivan County District Attorney was being pressed to undertake a grand jury investigation. Questions were being raised about the large quantities of drugs that had reportedly been consumed at the Festival. A newspaper reported that I was involved in a large drug operation, one of its reporters having discovered the source of my inheritance and jumped to the wrong conclusions. Toothpaste and denture cleaners make feeble hallucinogens. There was a great public outcry. Children of prominent people had returned home spaced out, tripping, exhausted, and gibbering. The *Times* ran a stern reprimand of an editorial calling us reckless and irresponsible.

The worst thing initially was the uncertainty. Would the Bank honor the line of credit? Until we knew that, we couldn't meet payrolls, fund the cleanup, pay rent, or anything. Of course, everyone who thought we needed to be told let us know that we owed them money, and some of our creditors were heavies who weren't likely to confine themselves to piercing corporate veils. Michael and Artie left town shortly after the Festival, riding the wave of notoriety the event had generated for them. In some circles, I guess, they were even lionized. When they finally returned to New York, we negotiated an end to our partnership with them. It was painful.

We turned the corner in the chaos department when the Bank decided to fund our reorganization. Checks were honored. Workers were paid. Defense lawyers were hired. Accountants returned. Rent was paid. We could find out where we stood financially, and then, we hoped, do something about it. It turned out that we had some assets after all. Wadleigh had shot a movie, and the word from him and from the people at Warner Brothers was that it was dynamite. Recordings had also been made. Moreover, having a name and a logo of some value in the youth market, we were able to strike a deal with a licensing outfit.

The movie deal, though providential, wasn't all gravy. Artie had negotiated it with Wadleigh and Warners at the last minute. In an effort to get the damn thing to happen, he had agreed to just about everything they asked for. In typical Woodstock fashion, he had been over a barrel. In Kornfeld fashion, he had returned with a contract that was totally impossible to honor. We were in breach the moment he signed it, in fact. We had warranted that we either had or could get releases from all the artists who were to be filmed. We had not and we could not. There were other things we had agreed to supply, such as licenses and permits and money, none of which could be forthcoming. Our lawyers advised us that our one chance lay in the film being a blockbuster. In that case, Warners, in their eagerness to release it, would do themselves those things that we were supposed to have done for them. Breach or no breach, they couldn't release the movie without our approval. They came and made us a generous offer for our share of the rights. We accepted.

Then there was the bad press we got. In addition to the *Times* editorial, there was an article in *Business Week* that likened our corporate setup and procedures to a Walt Disney cartoon. The underground papers had a field day. They charged us with ripping off everyone in sight. Things gradually got better, however. The word got out that everyone had had a good time. The *Times* wrote another editorial calling Woodstock "A Phenomenon of Innocence." Al Aronowitz in the *Post* wrote a really nice story about me and my family; how we had lost so much money and still honored our obligations. Once it became known that we had truly taken a bath, we stopped looking evil and began to look merely foolish. To some people we even looked good. They were impressed that we had been responsible for something that had generated so much excitement, interest, and comment. I was actually sought after, congratulated, and admired now and then, although I couldn't for the life of me understand why. As far as I was concerned, the whole experience had become a colossal embarrassment. There were seventy separate legal proceedings pending against us, after all.

In October, Max Yasgur's friends gave him a testimonial dinner for bringing the great Woodstock Bonanza to Sullivan County. Joel and I attended as guests of honor. We listened to speeches extolling Max's decency, his foresight, and his contributions to the community. People greeted us like heroes, like bearers of manna. Many wanted to know if we would consider doing the whole thing again in 1970!

A year after the Festival, a local newspaper up near the site proposed that a historical marker be erected there to commemorate what had taken place. Two years later, just before the statute of limitations ran out, we were sued by the Town of White Lake for having disturbed the peace and having caused property damage.

I sometimes wonder if I'll ever see the end of it.

PROFIT (?) AND LOSS (!): DECEMBER 31, 1973

LAND: None

STAFF: Renee

TICKET RECEIPTS: $1,800,000

OTHER RECEIPTS: $ 1,500,000 (movie, record, licensing, etc.)

TOTAL RECEIPTS: $3,300,000

TALENT BOOKINGS: Talent cost $250,000

ATTORNEYS: One in New York City. Large alumni association meets annually in the Grand Ballroom of the Waldorf Astoria

PORTABLE TOILETS: One still missing

MONEY SPENT: $2,800,000

POST-FESTIVAL EXPENSES: $600,000 (lawsuits, settlements, accountants, staff, interest charges, psychotherapy)

TOTAL EXPENSES: $3,400,000

PROFIT (LOSS): ($100,000)

ROBERTS AND ROSENMAN REFLECT

John

After the Festival, well-meaning friends told me that with the passage of time I would see Woodstock for what it really was: a kind of cultural Camelot, peopled by beautiful and kindly moppets. They told me that my feelings of aversion sprang from being "too close to it." I needed distance. Well, here I am, half a decade distant; and so, a few thoughts.

Woodstock, the event, was a coincidence. It happened that our concept of peace, music, and remote rural vistas struck an extremely responsive chord in most American kids. Many powerful trends converged to generate our mammoth audience and to keep it peaceful and happy. The first trend was the sense of community that young people were developing. The second trend was musical, the elevation to demigoddom of rock stars. With music, kids could fulfill their fantasies of success, sexual conquest, and mass approval by watching contemporaries, very easy to identify with, act them out. At Woodstock, for example, the performers and the crowd were almost one. The third trend was dropping out. We advertised a community of youth. For a few dollars admission—if you were among the few who bothered to buy tickets—you got a place to live among your own kind, away from most of life's hassles, especially the folks. You got a Peter Pan fantasy, a never-never land peopled by kid stars, kid storekeepers, and kid police. It was an irresistible lure: a world without adults or authority where one never had to grow up.

The crowd wanted it to work. If it worked, it was real. There was a feeling that the Establishment had to be shown. The Generation was on trial and, by God, it was going to be found innocent and taken seriously.

I embarked on the Woodstock project as an investment. It was my belief that a good idea, properly funded and competently handled, would be a winner. It was also my belief that Joel and I, between us, could recognize good ideas, estimate eventual costs, and manage ventures with intelligence. I prided myself on my ability to judge character as well, and the only explanation I can offer for all this unwarranted self-confidence is ignorance. What you don't know can't intimidate you. Success in business—or just about anything, for that matter—requires, in addition to luck, brains, and money, a generous sprinkling of thoroughness and attention to detail. I was having too much fun to stop and pay those necessary dues when Woodstock first got rolling. It was all a great lark. Without ever admitting it to myself, I was out to prove that success could be had without toil and fulfillment without commitment. I was, in short, arrogant and foolish—and wrong.

But I was lucky. In the first place, I survived. My ego, to be sure, was bruised, my fortunes diminished, my plans in ashes. But I rescued my self-esteem in the very act of surviving. It took a lot of careful planning and hard work, but I managed it, and the best part was that I was able to learn from my mistakes. Today, I usually know what I'm doing. More important, I recognize when I don't.

Finally, I have withstood some grueling challenges and come through—to my own satisfaction, at least—as a decent and honorable person. I have faced the fact that there are limitations to my abilities, but I have concluded that that still leaves an adequate human being. I like my ability to grow and learn, and I expect to continue doing both. To my surprise, I have become pretty hard-working and thorough, qualities I have always mistrustfully admired in my father. I guess my rebellion is over. I give Woodstock a good part of the credit for that.

Joel

After the Festival, somebody got it into his noggin that Woodstock had been a phenomenon. It's comforting to have phenomenon status. Phenomenons may lose money and still be respected entries in encyclopedias. They may be sloppily organized and administered without embarrassing their progenitors. Also, phenomenons give the people associated with them a sense of having participated in something larger than life.

I didn't think that I was setting out on a joy ride when I signed the papers with Michael, Artie, and Jock in February of 1969. I anticipated hard work and began under the illusion that I had the capacity to pull the project off. At the time, I was wrong. But panic has a way of making an avid student of me. A year from that February, I was a hundred years older—and even a little wiser.

I've always been the type who's fine during a crisis but who then disintegrates when the pressure eases. By December of 1969, the Woodstock Crisis, for me at least, was still in full swing. Sometime in 1970 I began to see daylight, and, of course, began to get depressed because I wasn't operating on emergency power any more. At the very time when Woodstock discussions were most frequent, I had the least tolerance for anything associated with it.

On the Monday following the Festival, the New York *Times* printed an editorial entitled "Nightmare in the Catskills." The following day, in an unprecedented reversal, they printed an editorial called "Morning After at Bethel," which was virtually a paean to the Woodstock experience. What took the *Times* two days took me about two years. In 1969 and 1970, Nightmare in the Catskills seemed a pretty fair description. By 1971, though, I was beginning to feel faint stirrings of what I came later to identify as pride. Soon I was ready to talk about the Festival with friends. And I had a lot to say. After all, it wasn't just any old weekend in the country; it was a phenomenon.

Woodstock Music and Art Fair	Woodstock Music and Art Fair	Woodstock Music and Art Fair	THREE DAY TICKET
FRIDAY	**SATURDAY**	**SUNDAY**	
August 15, 1969 10 A. M.	August 16, 1969 10 A. M.	August 17, 1969 10 A. M.	Aug. 15, 16, 17 1969
$6.00	**$6.00**	**$6.00**	
Good For One Admission Only	Good For One Admission Only	Good For One Admission Only	**$18.00**
86038 NO REFUNDS	86038 NO REFUNDS	86038 NO REFUNDS	86038

**"YOUNG MEN WITH UNLIMITED CAPITAL
LOOKING FOR INTERESTING, LEGITIMATE INVESTMENT
OPPORTUNITIES AND BUSINESS PROPOSITIONS."**
THE NEW YORK TIMES, 3/22/67

It started with this ad, placed by Joel Rosenman and John Roberts
as a way to find interesting work after college. It led
Rosenman and Roberts to stage a gathering that changed the face of popular
culture: the Woodstock Music and Art Fair in August 1969.
Woodstock is rightly remembered as the pivotal event that united a
generation, but the behind-the-scenes story is less utopian—
and absolutely fascinating.

Rosenman and Roberts describe their shock as they realized,
after a long struggle to find a site and placate area residents, that the
festival was attracting a crowd ten times larger than expected,
stalling traffic for miles around, and forcing thousands of ticket
holders to be turned away. The instant city of Woodstock created
mind-boggling logistical problems for Rosenman and Roberts:
mud, shortages of food, water, and medical help, a death, births, bad
drugs—and waking up their local banker in the middle of the
night to get $15,000 for The Who and the Grateful Dead, who refused
to go onstage without cash in their pockets.

By the time Jimi Hendrix played "The Star-Spangled Banner"
at 6:30 Monday morning, there were "only" 25,000 people left, but
Rosenman and Roberts faced a sea of mud and trash, irate neighbors,
bad press ("Nightmare in the Catskills"), staggering debts, and some
seventy separate legal proceedings against them. But the ultimate
impact of that weekend was far greater—and far more triumphal for
all involved. *Young Men with Unlimited Capital* is an amazing story:
a crucial document for understanding America in the 1960s.